Latter-day Saints and the Bible

A Comparative Study

Brian Grant Kent

ISBN: 1-4781-3889-0
ISBN-13: 9781478138891
Library of Congress Control Number: 2012912123

Dedication

To the mountains and trees! And if there are no trees, then to the mountains! If there are no mountains then there is no point. I might as well have a stupid car.

Contents

Introduction

Most LDS literature tries to proclaim the Restored Gospel and express the testimonies of the members of the Church of Jesus Christ of Latter-day Saints. We try to avoid studying and preaching against other people's religions because it spawns prejudice. But it is important to know and understand the traditions of religions to see how they affect the hearts and minds of those who believe in them and today it's important to understand why the Restored Gospel supports and denies many of these traditions. Regretfully I'm not able to go very deep into these traditions as some might expect, I've only produced concise overviews of the issues so as not to get bogged down with the details, sort of like explaining the game of football in 120 words or less.

The Gospel of Jesus Christ comforts the afflicted and afflicts the comfortable. To effectively combat the enemy you must know what he knows. So I've taken great time and effort to research the histories of traditional Christianity and demonstrate how many of them have been based on the understandings of mortal minds and evolved into practices and principles that are not accepted by Jesus Christ. Through comparative study we can see why there was a need for a restoration of the Gospel rather than another reformation.

Satan attacks us through our weak spots, the fact that we do not make it a practice to study and teach other people's religions within the walls or our Church makes us relatively ignorant to the tactics of the adversary, but it doesn't mean we can't study on our own through prayer and faith. One of Captain Moroni's virtues as a warrior was that he was always one step ahead of the enemy, he used espionage to gain information valuable to his own defenses, and he saw it no sin to defend their livelihoods through stratagem. We must always try to defend our portion of the battle line and we hope to be inspired by a better cause. If we are as smart as the enemy then we can defeat them, we cannot be lateral in facing a multi-faceted enemy, and where there is one with courage then there is the majority.

Hopefully I can be direct and truthful without being antagonistic. No doubt some people will be offended, I don't think that can be avoided, people have been offended over lesser things. People were offended by Jesus Christ and He was about as direct and truthful as a person can get. I pray always that I can write with the spirit of truth and not get caught up with the spirit of contention as it seems to be a natural tendency. Hopefully these things can add to the links of righteous armor for the individual.

As with most authors, I write so I can hopefully inspire people, enlighten their minds, and bring about a mighty change in their lives, but better yet, to become mandatory reading at colleges and universities and charge triple-digit prices for my book. Now *that's* living the dream!

Chapter 1: The Anthropomorphic God

Working the oil fields; now, that is an experience to be treasured. Everything is covered in dirt, grease and mud, and the air is filled with the lingering odor of diesel exhaust (when an inversion sets in you can almost choke to death.) Everyone drives a four-wheel-drive and they're all covered with mud and all the men wear dirty overalls, grease stained gloves and scratched up hard hats from throwing them on the ground and kicking them. We cuss the weather, we cuss the equipment, and sometimes we cuss each other. I worry that the Lord's gonna call me on that one and say, 'You know, Brian, you never did fix that cussing streak, did you?' Well, I was busy, dang it. Then somebody in a shiny, new SUV shows up wearing shiny, new jeans and a shiny, new button down shirt and proceeds to tell us what needs to be done. It's enough to put anyone in a fighting mood. We all know we're in this world together and we're doing the best we can with what we've got. Nothing is more frustrating than somebody with power and authority so completely removed from the operation. And then there is God.

An anthropomorphic god is one who has human qualities. Jews believe God is not anthropomorphic in any possible way, that he has no will to reveal to mankind, and we are not his children as that would give him an undesirable human quality. To Jews and Muslims, God is beyond the limits of human comprehension, and to Catholics God is uncreated and unknowable. The same attitude is shared among Protestant religions. As Latter-day Saints we believe God is very anthropomorphic. I'd like to demonstrate how Greek mythology greatly influenced the refulgent spirit god concept, how Joseph Smith's First Vision changed centuries of faulty tradition, and that God is knowable to each person who desires to know Him.

It is Greek mythology that teaches that the spirit is more powerful than the physical, that God must be a spirit to hold reign over the resurrected Christ, and this philosophy was adopted right along with Trinitarianism when the Nicene Creed was written and the Catholic Church was established, and these things passed right on through the Protestant religions. This concept was written into the early Greek texts that now make up the New Testament. So it should be no surprise that Christian apologists emphatically point to the scripture that states, *God is a spirit: and they that worship him must worship him in spirit and in truth (John 4:24.)* But there seems to be some incongruity here, the passage refers to the manner in which people are to worship God, and every other passage in the Bible which refers to God implies He has a body, parts and passions, and a gender. History has shown that myths (stories originating within traditions) and mysteries (something not fully understood or that baffles or eludes understanding) have certain power over people, and accompany many worldly views of God.

Joseph Smith, having seen for himself the true nature of God knew this passage couldn't be true, and being a prophet commissioned to make corrections in the Bible restated the verse to read, *For unto such hath God promised his Spirit. And they who worship him, must worship in spirit and in truth (Joseph Smith Translation John 4:26.)* This simple change makes a world of difference in belief structure. Joseph Smith's First Vision in 1820 established that God has a physical and tangible body defying centuries of traditional teaching. In later revelations Brother Joseph declared that God underwent the same creative process as us, thus having a unique perspective on the human condition, and demonstrated the potential that mortal men have for the eternities. We even found out God has a name. Furthermore, it has been revealed that

God has a home planet, being a god having a real, physical body he also has a real, physical home, the same as we have been promised in this earth. All these things bring the connections with God more intimate and clear, the unknowable becomes knowable, and what is mysterious to other becomes enlightenment. It isn't a true God who creates confusion in the ranks of mankind, it is the theologies of mankind that do that.

Knowing God is possible, and we can know as much about Him as we want, the resources are available and we can pray and receive answers that establish a special connection with Him. Knowing God isn't about knowing about Him through scripture study and the preached word, although that helps, but we can know for ourselves that the things we are taught are true. We are admonished to study and pray and learn these things so that we can have our own understanding of heavenly things. Mankind is nothing compared to the greatness of God's creations, but we matter to Him, and we are taught four divine principles concerning His love for us; 1) God loves the humble and meek, 2) He trusts the fullness of the Gospel to the weak and simple to proclaim to the ends of the earth, 3) no matter where a person lives or how humble their circumstances, we are not invisible to Him, and 4) what hardships we might experience in this world will not last forever. As mere mortal men we cannot comprehend God in His fullest, but God is not beyond us, all we need to do is reach out to Him.

Our God is not one of seclusion and hidden from mankind, nor is He secretive and aloof, but He wants us to know Him. The human qualities that God possesses are qualities that we humans can obtain and be rewarded in the future. Nearly every major religion of the world believes God is a refulgent spirit existing in all things, but we have eyewitness accounts that say otherwise, and we have the Holy Ghost to manifest the truth of these things.

It is admirable that so many good Christians hold the Bible with such great reverence and respect, to believe that it is a manifestation of God's word and is perfect and inerrant in its messages, and to stand boldly in upholding its Gospel message. Many use it as the anchor for their beliefs and swear upon its teachings. It is most admirable. Our friends in other churches try so hard to hold to what they have in a world that bombards them with so much fraud and deceit, it is understandable that they should be afraid of the absurd concepts of our Church, but it is those who make them afraid who are at fault.

Chapter 2: Baptism by Water

I wanted to go to Maggie's Café today, I had never been to this town before and I felt in the mood for hash browns and eggs, but she was closed up. I drove all over town several times trying to find a place that wasn't a national franchise, something that wasn't already in the last town I was in, a place that wasn't so familiar and common. In a small town I expect to find a café or diner named after the founder or owner who also runs the place and will come out and visit with you, and has pictures of the family and their vacation trips all over the walls, and maybe the heads of animals they shot, and they cook food they way they like to cook it. A place with personality, unlike any other place on earth, and a place where the locals go to sit around the liars' table every day and the waitress doesn't have to ask what they want because they've been around long enough to know what they like and don't care for anything else. A town is a home and I like to go where the family eats. I stood in front of Maggie's for several minutes and realized she hadn't been open for some time now. I suppose if a man's *gotta* eat he can always go to national franchise.

Baptism is another thing that separates us from other churches. There are as many ways to baptize a person as there are churches throughout the world. Yet, the Apostles declared that there was *One Lord, one faith, one baptism (Eph. 4:5.)* Latter-day Saints believe this to be literal, that there is only one method for baptism as revealed by the Lord, and any deviation from that method is null. It is apparent that the variations of baptism evolved with traditions, that true baptism must be revealed and that strict adherence must be observed.

Many Christian theologians are starting to believe that baptism was performed by the ancient Jews in the Old Testament, although it's not plainly stated, Jews did hold ritual washings by immersion similar to baptism. John the Baptist is credited as being one of the first people recorded for baptizing with authority along with the Apostles of Jesus Christ. It is disputed among scholars how important Jesus' baptism principle was and whether he intended it to continue through an organized church. After the death of the Apostles we find Christianity branching out with different teachings and baptismal methods, and by the 4th century well known styles included triple baptism, infant baptism, pouring water over the head, and sprinkling water on the head. The purpose of baptism varies as much as the meanings and the importance of baptism is always in question. It is clear that when the Apostles died they took the Priesthood authority and the doctrine of baptism with them, from there the orthodoxy went where ever the local theology took it, and up until 1829 baptism was entirely whatever men wanted it to be.

In May of 1829, while translating the Book of Mormon, Joseph Smith and Oliver Cowdery came upon a passage describing baptism, so they went into the woods to pray and inquire. In answer, John the Baptist appeared and administered to them giving them authority and instructions on proper baptism. They went to the river and Joseph baptized Oliver, and then vice versa, making Oliver Cowdery the first man baptized with authority since the days of the Apostles. That authority has been passed down through generations of worthy men, and now spread throughout the world, even to this old cowboy. Of all the methods of baptism in all the churches, only one is done according to revealed doctrine.

Because the doctrine of baptism has been revealed, so has the principle, and it is very strict. First, we believe that baptism is absolutely mandatory for a person to inherit the highest heaven (*John 3:5,*) so important that Jesus Christ himself was required to do so (*Matt. 3:15,*) and not just as a demonstration of obedience. Second, we believe that baptism must be administered by an authorized Priesthood holder otherwise the ordinance is null and void, as a result baptisms performed by ministers of other churches are completely ineffective and must be performed again when becoming a member of the Church of Jesus Christ of Latter-day Saints. Third, we believe that every ordinance in the Church is coupled with a covenant and when a person breaks the covenant they can be ex-communicated from the Church and need re-baptism to re-establish that covenant. Fourth, as a revealed covenant and ordinance it is very specific in which the ordinance is performed and the prayer recited, they must be administered in exacting detail otherwise the ordinance must be performed again, as it is not a requirement set forth by man but from God it must be done His way. Fifth, every person who has ever lived must receive the baptismal ordinance to enter the highest heavens, those who died never having the opportunity must have that work done vicariously in the temple, and there are no exceptions *(1 Cor. 15:29.)*

We are a peculiar people, there is no question about that, but we do what we know to be right in spite of criticism we might receive for it. There can be countless baptisms as there are churches, but there can only be one true baptism established through revelation, and only one true faith. The traditions of men have brought forth numerous reasons and methods, the restored Gospel has brought back the true order, and we have found it to be exacting and detailed.

The Christian religions through history have made efforts to keep the holy rite sacred in their traditions, and without question it is an exciting and joyous time for all those involved in the baptism, and there is always a sense of welcoming acceptance in the congregation. Regardless of the varying views on baptism it seems almost universally accepted among Christendom that baptism is a sacred ordinance that brings a person closer to God.

Chapter 3: Baptism by Fire

My old Jeep is just giving me a heck of a time, it won't start right, and I'll be dipped if I can figure out why. I've replaced everything from the battery to the starter (lots of shiny parts, now) and it still won't start right. All my gut instinct tells me I don't know what I'm doing. But I keep tinkering, I've got a few weeks before springs settles in, and there can be only so many things wrong before I'll trip the right trigger. Then I'll head for the mountains and nobody will see the Grey Ghost for a while. In the meantime I sit and think, and sometimes I just sit.

Following baptism is confirmation into the Church and receiving the Gift of the Holy Ghost.

Without revelation we cannot know the existence of God (as He could be a figment of imagination,) the true ministry of Jesus Christ (and He could be just another wise teacher,) the truths written in the Bible (otherwise it's just print on page,) that Joseph Smith was a true prophet of God (just look on the internet and you'll find plenty of comments on that,) and that this is the true Church of Jesus Christ. The Holy Ghost is so vital in revelation, it is by the power of the Holy Ghost that we can know all truth concerning the Kingdom of Heaven, and even angels speak by the power of the Holy Ghost. The mainstream views of the Holy Ghost are explained in the most divers ways, but it is only through the Holy Ghost that we can know the realm of God's creations, and he can be with us during our most trying times.

The main problem with most of Christianity is that they try to determine how a trinity can be a unity. The Bible clearly states, *Thou shalt have not other gods before me. (Ex. 20:3.)* The Old Testament teaches monotheism, or the worship of one god, while the New Testament teaches of the Father, the Son and the Holy

Ghost. Most churches teach one of two doctrines concerning this; 1) that all three are the same god acting out different parts, or 2) all three are the parts of the sum, just like the body, the engine and the tires make one car. The Holy Ghost (most often referred to as the Holy Spirit) is the most diminished of the three, often viewed as proceeding from the Father and Son, sometimes not even as a personage but an energy or active force (like *Star Wars,* I guess,) and it is becoming more popular that the Holy Ghost isn't even a part of the Trinity.

For us the Holy Ghost isn't just a mystery entity being credited as a member of the Trinity, or an essence of the character of God, but a real spirit being of personality and character sharing authority and power as a member of the Godhead. He is the testator who manifests the truth of all things, the one who communicates to us through revelation, and the only one in which mere mortal man can receive communication on a regular basis. We also believe we can have the privilege of the Holy Ghost being a constant companion, most commonly called the *Gift of the Holy Ghost,* and after baptism we are confirmed as members of the Church and commanded to receive the Holy Ghost. This special gift allows us to grow spiritually as He helps us to make decisions in difficult situations and helps us to know we've made correct choices. When we make poor choices He lets us know when we have repented adequately and are forgiven so we can move on with our lives. He inspires us when we need help solving difficult problems and comforts us in bad situations.

The Holy Ghost is not a substitute for common sense, he's not going to "inspire" us to do things we already know we should be doing, like going to Church and paying our tithing. He's not going to prompt us to choose fish over T-bone steak or what color of socks to wear. Unless it's a dire situation we're completely unaware of then he usually won't interrupt our daily lives. But if we make ourselves sensitive to the promptings of the spirit we can be prepared to recognize those promptings and have an added edge on a situation when it's needed. Our Heavenly Father has given us many things to redeem us from the Fall of Adam, but the Holy Ghost is our own personal guide through life who can bring us safely back to His presence, and the Gift of the Holy Ghost is the greatest gift given to mankind which brings all the graces of God and the righteous works of mankind together to the point of full salvation. So important is this ordinance that it is also given through vicarious temple work to those who have passed on, strangely, even in their present condition they cannot know of spiritual things without the aid of the Holy Ghost.

As human beings we are hardly worthy to receive direct contact from angels or Jesus Christ, and certainly not from Our Heavenly Father. But we are worthy to receive manifestations from the Holy Ghost. The Holy Ghost is the means we can know all things pertaining to the Kingdom of Heaven, the Gift of the Holy Ghost is the very same baptism of fire mentioned by our Savior, and his powerful impressions burn in the soul more effectively than all the open visions of ancient prophets. The varying views of the Holy Ghost is mostly guess work because the Bible tends to be vague on the matter, but we can know all things in the Kingdom of Heaven by the Holy Ghost, and his companionship creates a link between ourselves and deity.

Many churches recognize the Holy Ghost as part of the Trinity and try very hard to understand the relationship of Him with the other members of the Godhead. The explanations of how the Trinity is a unity and how they work together are interesting and creative. Their traditions have left colorful and profound histories that have been inspiring examples of how to overcome extreme adversity. We can't deny that the Holy Ghost prompted many of the Christian reformers to break away from Orthodoxy; we can't deny people felt the powerful urges to seek religious freedom in the New World, and we certainly can't deny that the writers of the U.S. constitution were inspired to guarantee religious freedom. Our friends in other churches have left rich and lasting legacies that have paved the way for the Restored Gospel and they deserve our gratitude.

Chapter 4: Living Prophets

Comic book heroes seem to be the kick these days, the stories are simple with the good guys clearly defined, and they have moral messages. Back in the '50's and '60's it was the Biblical figures who were who were the big screen heroes, and the '70's produced the "anti-hero" like *Dirty Harry,* in whom the good guy is just badder than the bad guys. But I wonder if a truly good person, one who deserves to be admired by others, is one who is complimented by Jesus. Of John the Baptist our Savior said was the greatest prophet of all time. The Lord made frequent occasion to quote Isaiah, and they say it's one thing to quote the Lord but quite another to be quoted by the Lord. In this day and age the moral dilemmas tug at people's consciences with questions on who to believe in and who not to, looking back I think the Biblical character I admire the most, someone I'd like to be like, is Nathanial, in whom the Lord said, *an Israelite indeed, in whom there is no guile. (John 1:47)*

Every prophet ever recorded in the Bible has been a true and living prophet, each one was a modern day prophet for his time, and people bore witness to the truthfulness of their callings. Each prophet has brought forth a dispensation, or the dispensing of the knowledge of God to the people, and each prophet has received revelation from on High. Our belief in deity, our baptism, our views on the Holy Ghost, and our belief in living prophets are the most prominent differences that separate ours from other Christian religions. The methods in which others establish doctrine and their attitudes towards prophets are completely contrary to our dependency of revelation from on High.

In churches where Pastors teach against Priesthood organization, that each congregation is autonomous governance, we find those Pastors declaring the word of God according to the traditions and theologies they have accepted and studied. The views of each Pastor may vary from others as their sermons are developed through research of scripture, history, ethnics and philosophy to establish explanations for the things we find in the Bible. Sometimes doctrinal matters become a contest of opinions. Others refer to the orthodoxy and creeds of the Dark Ages as the foundations of their beliefs. Many of those practices have slowly changed. Others interpret the written text of the Bible through literature, religion and law encompassing forms of communication to include the written, verbal and nonverbal. This is to establish coherent explanations on Biblical concepts considered vague to the average reader. This is not dispensation of the word of God and these are not the ways true religion is established.

It seems that prophets of old are now just mythological creatures. All the western or Abrahamic religions believe in prophets of old but very few believe in modern day prophets. Christian views are pretty vague, some profess that anyone who even claims to be a prophet is a false prophet, while others admit the possibilities of living prophets but don't adhere to any. Some claim the prophets ended with the Old Testament allowing only John the Baptist and Jesus Christ after that. Many feel that Jesus Christ fulfilled all righteousness and therefore we require no more dispensation of faith. Others say that people since Christ's time have been more righteous than before and do not need prophets to lead them, and that the proclaimed word of God from His scriptures is all that is needed to direct people in righteousness. The American Restoration Movement began efforts in the early 1800's to restore church organizations to Christ's organization, and many will claim that Mormonism was part of that movement, but we have very few similarities to those organizations and they don't make any claim to the use of prophets in their restoration work.

Of the things I've mentioned so far, this may be one of the most prominent issues that separate Mormonism from other forms of Christianity; the fact that Joseph Smith was called of God to be a prophet, in ways similar to ancient prophets, was assisted by open visions and dispensations of knowledge and doctrine completely new to the minds of modern man. Each successor in the Presidency of the Church has also been regarded as a Prophet and has received revelation concerning the growth of the Church and the concerns of its people, and to act as a voice to the entire world the declarations of God. Each of the Apostles are considered prophets, seers, and revelators in being special witnesses of Christ and all of the General Authorities (to include the First Presidency, the Apostles, and the Seventy) are prophets to govern the affairs of the Church. All lay-office holders are given the rights of prophecy to govern their offices and areas of responsibility. We also teach that all people can be prophets in their own degrees of responsibility concerning their spiritual growth and journey back to our Heavenly Father. We believe in prophecy and we teach how prophecy is received and understood, with these things we understand how ancient prophets worked, and we know they weren't just mythological creatures with magical powers.

It is because of the modern day and living prophets that The Church of Jesus Christ of Latter-day Saints is a living church through continuous revelation unlike a Protestant or an Orthodox Church, or a dead branch from a dead tree. Our belief in living prophets is probably the most important thing in our Church that separates us from others as everything we believe in is founded on revelation. The traditions of Christianity have assumed that doctrine is established through philosophy and tradition, and they have abolished prophets completely, and yet our Church from its very beginning has placed the greatest emphasis on the need for modern day and living prophets.

Take a look around, watch the news for a half hour, and listen to the popular music produced. Can anyone honestly say that people in general are better than in ancient times? With mass communication and on-demand, on-line information, and the world at your fingertips, can anyone truly say we don't need inspiration and direction from the heavens? Are we wiser for our technology or are we becoming slaves to it? Presently I sit at a café tapping out my thoughts while waiting for my car to get out of the shop. I think we live in the most incredible time in history, but my soul desires to be in the mountains away from the wiles of society, so I can share my heart and my mind with my Maker.

Chapter 5: Between the Eternities

I have a new favorite Western, *Broken Trail, 2006,* starring Robert Duvall and Thomas Haden Church. A small team of cowboys run a herd of horses from Oregon to Wyoming and take into their care five young Chinese girls. The scenery alone makes it worth watching and every time I see the shots of the Grand Tetons and the Snake River I feel the urge to take a road trip. While on the trail two of the girls meet untimely and tragic deaths and Duvall's character recites these brief but profound words, *We're all travelers in this world, from the sweet grass to the packing house. Birth 'till death, we travel between the eternities.*

Often it seems Mormons are passive when it comes to the sciences involving the origin of man. In the battle between science and religion more Christian apologists are coming forward to defend the teachings of the Bible and refute the theories that might corrode the faith of their people. It seems that we are not as fervent on the issue as others, but we are creationists. Scientific theories provide explanations that help people understand the possibilities of their origins, but our Heavenly Father has provided truths concerning our origins as part of an over-all creation plan, and we can use much of the scientific discoveries to aid in our efforts to do the Lord's work.

The basis of Evolution rides on the theory that all living organisms developed through time and circumstance from one common organism. It is generally accepted that the first reproducing proteins developed about 3.7 billion years ago and have produced all living organisms we have today. Species and divergences of life are inferred from shared sets of similar traits or shared DNA sequences, such as rats and mice or man and apes, which share more recent ancestry. Evolutionary histories can be reconstructed using existing species and fossil records, and patterns of diversity can be shaped by speciation (development of species) and extinction. While many theories of organic evolution have cultivated through the ages, Charles Darwin was the first to formulate a scientific argument by means of natural selection, a process inferring three facts about populations: 1) the excess of population supported by the environment, 2) traits varying in individuals causing different rates of survival and reproduction, and 3) the hereditary traits passed through the generations. There is a great deal more to be said on the matter but we can't do that in this book.

Latter-day Saints are creationists. We believe that we are the product of design by deity. All men and women are literally from God *(Gen. 2:7, 22,)* begotten by heavenly parents as spirit beings before being made in the flesh *(Zech. 12:1,)* then coming to earth with the potential to become like our Heavenly Father and receive all He has *(1 John 3:2.)* We believe that mortality is only one part of the creation process; first as spirit children living with our Heavenly Father, then as mortals who receive physical bodies and gain experiences that further our development, followed by the resurrection in which spirit and body are joined permanently *(Rev. 20:6,)* and then to receive our eternal rewards *(Rev. 21:7.)* We are literally traveling between the eternities. We believe Adam and Eve were our first mortal parents and that their fall allowed for procreation and free agency to choose between good and evil *(Gen 3:22.)* We also believe that all animals were created in their respective spheres, or complete species, after the earth was prepared for life and shortly before mankind *(Gen. 1:24.)* We believe that earth was in a state of paradise before the fall of Adam and will be returned to that state after the Second Coming of Christ *(Ps. 104:30.)* And we have three sets of scripture to testify of these things; the Book of Genesis, the Book of Moses, and the Book of Abraham.

We don't spend much time and effort refuting the theory of evolution because we understand that the theory itself is based on the reasoning of man, but the scientific findings related to evolution is absolutely incredible. The most valuable resource surfacing from evolutionary experiments is the mapping of genes and DNA. We have found that genetic mapping can be used for family history and ancestry. Genetic history gives people a chance to check results from DNA testing to link themselves with other living relatives, determine ancestral homeland, validate existing research, confirm or deny connections between families, and prove or disprove theories regarding ancestry. Genetic mapping can measure a person's precise connections to indigenous ethnic groups from around the world. It provides deep group comparisons dating back more than 1000 years and individual comparisons for less than 1000 years. We're just scratching the surface of what is possible with this remarkable tool. Unfortunately, genetic mapping holds a similar problem with scriptures, the press and the public tend to extrapolate more than what is scientifically possible or appropriate to state as valid conclusions.

We don't openly oppose scientists in their pursuits of the origins of mankind as much as other Christian apologists. As a principle we know that we are the creatures of a divine being, the details are somewhat vague at times, but it's more important that we know our true origins so we're not caught up with the dizzying intellect of man. Scientific postulation provides people with explanations for the findings in the earth, living prophets have revealed the true nature of our origin and the plans for our creation, and we can make use of the many scientific discoveries to help further the work of the Lord.

We don't feel that scientists are enemies of the Church. We like scientists, we like being scientist; most scientists have religious beliefs and find that their discoveries do not contend with their faiths, and most all scientists are working for common goals. The scientific theories are efforts to explain evidence in ways that do not include religion because of the biasness of religions, religious people are always trying to snag evidence to prove their religion right, and many organizations that fund research will not support religious based science groups for the same reason. Scientific theories are just that, theories. We feel very confident in our convictions and don't feel threatened by discoveries of science, as we believe that all true science and all true religion are in harmony, *for the earth shall be full of the knowledge of the Lord, as the waters cover the sea. (Isaiah 11:9.)*

Chapter 6: The Mormon Cult

The 4th of July fell on a Sunday this year, and all the people in town threw a parade and celebrated while I went to Church and sang hymns of patriotism; *My Country 'Tis of Thee, God Bless America,* and *America the Beautiful.* Our speakers talked about what a cherished right we have been given through the Constitution which guarantees the freedom of worship and I reflected on how much it meant to me, as well. My non-denominational friends also went to their church that day, and they sang patriotic hymns, and their pastor preached of civil freedoms. I told them how glad I was that they did, I couldn't think of a better way to celebrate Independence Day than going to Church, and that every week we go to worship we celebrate the very thing our forefathers fought and died for. I am thankful that I can sit in front of the temple and write my feelings without fear of people throwing things at me or being persecuted by the government, I try to remember those who made this possible, and I try not to take it for granted by wasting the moment.

The Church of Jesus Christ of Latter-day Saints has been considered a cult for quite some time. As the term has become more popularized, the definition has become more broadened to include just about every religious, political, and scientific field out there. Cultism is a constant debate concerning the Church, but it isn't the definition of a cult that people fear, instead it's the negative implications cultism generates. In its broadest terms practically every organization is a cult, some cults have used fear and manipulation to keep control over their members, and some are counted as dangerous organizations requiring police supervision.

First, it is a group whose beliefs or practices are considered abnormal or bizarre, a system of ritual practices. This is true about our Church; almost everything we do is ritual practice, from home teaching to temple work, and the more we do it the better we get at it. That's the point. Many of the things that have been revealed to us concerning the Kingdom of Heaven are very abnormal and bizarre compared to Christian traditions, and this can be expected as pointed out in *1 Cor. 2:14.* The scientific fields would also be included since much of their research, methods and theories are pretty bizarre. In the 1940's all religious groups outside Catholic orthodoxy were considered cults. That means everything, including Protestant Christianity, would be cults. By these definitions, those same orthodox Christians who call others cults would also be cults. Furthermore, 65% of the U.S. population claim some form of Protestant Christianity, making them the largest cult following in America. And then there are the eastern religions who believe in reincarnation and strange gods with elephant heads and multiple arms and legs. Face it, this is a bizarre world.

Second; a particular system of religious worship, especially with reference to its rites and ceremonies; an instance of great veneration of a person, ideal, or thing, especially as manifested by a body of admirers; the object of such devotion; a group or sect bound together by veneration of the same thing, person, ideal, etc.; sociology, a group having a sacred ideology and a set of rites centering around their sacred symbols. Okay, that's us, too. Strangely, the things I've so far mentioned are not really considered cults, because there is a negative image applied to the cult. A cult is also a temporary fad or fashion characterized by its lack of organizational structure. That's definitely not us. Our Church is credited for being one of the most effective and efficient organizations in place today. Cults are also known for using devious psychological techniques to gain and control adherents. Upon many occasions I have heard of Mormons being brainwashed. It makes me wonder if they really understand what they're saying. Brainwashing is a form of mind control that is very real. It began during the Korean War when prisoners of war were tortured and subjected to sleep and sensory deprivation to gain control of the person's mind. It may be effective, but the results are very short lived, and the victims are aware of what happened to them. This is an ignorant and blatant accusation. Brain washing is a detectable condition and if it were true then legal repercussions would ensue.

Let's consider the actual cults who live up to the negative imagery applied to them. In 1997 the Heaven's Gate Group committed mass suicide believing their spirits would be taken aboard a UFO following the Hale-Bopp Comet and go to another level of human existence. In 1994 a three month old boy was ritually sacrificed by the Order of the Solar Temple in Canada because he was identified as the Anti-Christ. And then there was the Branch Davidian Seventh-Day Adventists in Waco, Texas who believed that David Koresh was a prophet to reproduce the House of David. The People's Temple of Jonestown, Guyana committed the largest mass suicide (912 people) in modern history. Each one of these involved the deception or manipulation of people with fear. In 2002 a book was released to help police understand extremist groups who would attack societies throughout the world. *Extremist Groups: An International Compilation of Terrorist Organizations, Violent Political Groups, and Issue-Oriented Militant Movements (Sean Hill and Richard H. Ward, 2002, ISBN 0-942511-73-5)* lists groups, leaders and headquarter locations and operations of over 200 organizations worldwide who pose violent threats to people and communities. This list of dangerous groups includes (but not limited to) Aryan Nations, Church of Scientology, Earth First!, Ku Klux Klan, Republic of Texas, Concerned Christians, Earth Liberation Front, and People for the Ethical Treatment of Animals (PETA.) But the Church of Jesus Christ of Latter-day Saints is not on this list. Apparently sending well-dressed young men door to door with Books of Mormon to read, ponder and pray about doesn't pose a public threat. Perhaps being honest, true, chaste, benevolent, virtuous, and doing good to all men doesn't count as dangerous intent. Go figure.

When people talk about Mormonism being a cult they usually have in mind the negative implications like cult horror films. In its broadest terms it includes every organization and people in existence. The most basic terms would include our Church right along with every other religion, in some cases extreme churches have used fear and manipulation to direct their members, and some have become menaces to society.

It is the negative implications that people want most to project about Mormons, to stir up fear and hatred in the hearts of the ignorant, and those who fear Mormons need others to be afraid with them. Most people are smarter than that.

Chapter 7: The Mormon Christian

The early fall weather has changed the colors of the trees and dropped a skiff of snow on the ground, the fun filled festivities of Halloween have passed and we gently move to the hallowed memories of fallen comrades, and our thoughts and feelings are touched by the reverence towards those veterans who fought and died to uphold and protect the rights and freedoms we hold to today. We are a country that loves our fighting country man, we honor those who stood valiantly for the cause of freedom and justice and paid the ultimate sacrifice, and our debts to these great men and women can never be repaid but we can erect memorials and keep them in our hearts and prayers. When we listen to the testimonies of surviving soldiers it is apparent they have no idea why their lives were spared and so many good people lost their lives, through their lives we can see that nobody hates war and bloodshed more than veterans, and nobody loves freedom and peace more than those who fought for it. War is the result of failed politics and why our countrymen have to pay the price for it is beyond me. I think if our civil leaders were to go and duke it out themselves we wouldn't have war, but I know that isn't true. Life, liberty and the pursuit of happiness is always established by the common men who fight for it.

Are Mormons Christians? This is the age-old question in which the resounding answer is yes...and no. It depends on who you talk to. There are hundreds of individualized guidelines and none of them are meant to be inclusive, they are designed to exclude people, and to proclaim who the true Christians are and who will go to hell. Many people will say they are Christians because they are saved and Mormons are not because we don't believe in the moment-of-confession-salvation thingy, but we don't worry much about it. The principles of the Gospel are inclusive to all who choose to follow them. There are many reasons why most people don't consider Mormons to be Christians, and many reasons why we do consider ourselves Christian, and if we look back we can see how many Christians today follow a similar pattern as the Jews of Christ's time.

We do not adhere to the orthodox traditions or creeds, nor do we follow a reformed version of the Gospel, therefore, we are not Catholic or Protestant. To them the answer is a resounding no. Some say we are not Christians because they think we reject the divinity of Christ, we claim that God has a wife, and we do proxy baptisms for Jews of the Holocaust. Some believe that we have done baptism by proxy for Holocaust victims such as Ann Frank, ruthless dictators as Adolph Hitler, other church leaders as Pope John Paul II, and fear we do it for the living against their will or awareness. Some claim Mormonism is an Abrahamic religion right alongside Judaism, Islam, and Christianity. Some feel Mormons are Christians socially and culturally but not theologically. Others feel we're not Christians because we don't accept the Bible as the only word of God, the inerrancy or infallibility of the Bible, or the traditionally accepted authority of the Bible. For some it's because we don't believe in the symbol of the cross. Others don't like how we believe in the Trinity as being three distinct beings instead of being united in substance and person in some incomprehensible way. Some are utterly miffed that we don't accept the baptisms of other churches to be valid, that we consider ours to be the only true Church of Jesus Christ. Some of these are actually true and some are just blatant accusations.

We do believe we are Christians and really hate it when people accuse us of not being so because it implies we don't believe in Christ. We have very deep and personal convictions in Christ. In the simplest definitions we find *Christian: of, pertaining to, or derived from Jesus Christ or His teachings. (Dictionary.com)* We believe in the Restored Gospel *(Matt. 17:11, Eph.1:10, Rev. 14:6,)* which brought back to existence what used to be, and can only be done through prophecy and revelation. We believe in Jesus Christ; the Only Begotten Son of God *(Mark 1:11,)* creator of the earth and its inhabitants *(Col.1:16,)* redeemer of the world *(John 3:16-17,)* established the atonement to pay the price of sin *(Matt. 26:42,)* died on the cross under judgment of men and resurrected to secure eternal life for all mankind *(1 Cor. 15:20-23,)* the author of salvation *(Heb. 2:5-18,)* the Redeemer of Israel *(Luke 1:68-73,)* the mediator between God and man *(1 Tim. 2:5,)* and having all rights and authority of God to act in His stead *(John 8:28.)* Through Jesus Christ the gospel, all saving truths, every edifying principle, every ordinance, every Priesthood authority and office, every key to the Priesthood, and all knowledge of the Kingdom of Heaven that ever has been and ever will be is revealed by Him through the power of the Holy Ghost. We believe more in Christ and about Christ because we have been given more knowledge of Christ. We are Christians with a resounding yes.

So the real question is, are we Christians to be counted among secular Christendom? This may be the resounding no we can all agree on. Back in the days of the Apostles a similar question could be applied, were Christians Jews to be counted among the Jews? Jews themselves had drifted time and again from true principles of the Gospel and when Jesus came they were far enough removed that the organization He established was practically a new religion. But Jesus was a Jew who went among the Jews to teach them the correct worship and the majority rejected Him. After His resurrection He instructed the Apostles to go among the gentiles and teach the Gospel. Jewish tradition and text still played a large role in the new Church and many of its members considered themselves to be Jews adopted into the House of Israel. The breaking away from most Jewish traditions and lineage demanded this new explosion of fanatics be called something else, and the term Christian began as a derogatory title. It's not so different with us, our Church leaders are still accused of all manner of deception and our missionaries still get cussed and called names that don't apply, but we've become more and more accepted throughout the world and our work steadily goes forward.

The point is, the exclusion from Christianity isn't based on what we believe but how we've departed from tradition. The principles of the Gospel are meant for everyone willing to follow them. Many people who claim that Mormons are not Christians, in spite of our efforts to clearly show that we are, follow the same efforts of exclusion as done in past times.

Identity seems to be the issue with Christianity, those who can be counted among the Lord's elite, and everyone wants to believe they are in the elite. It seems perfectly acceptable to have thousands of man-made churches using the Bible as a guideline and not so acceptable to have one true church established through revelation. Our friends in other churches are under great pressure these days to maintain that sense of identity that sets them apart from worldliness. As our church grows locally and worldwide there are greater concerns among the people that ministers have to cope with as tactfully as possible without being jerks. It isn't an easy thing to do and I feel many of them are doing pretty well. Still, there is that concern as to who will be accepted by the Lord and who will be ignored *(Matt. 7:22-23.)*

Chapter 8: Accuracy of the Bible

I heard a tele-evangistical pastor come right out and tell his audience that they should not read the King James Bible no matter what, that nobody today is able to understand Elizabethan writing from four hundred years ago, and that it would be better to learn Greek and study the original texts. I thought that could have been the dumbest thing I'd heard (and when you work around truck drivers you hear some pretty stupid stuff.) I feel confident in saying that every single word in the KJV is found in the dictionary and carefully defined, histories are published concerning the stories, and lots of wonderful people in the ministries are available to help. There is no reason anyone cannot understand the KJV.

Addressing the accuracy of the Bible proves to be a direct offense to those who believe it is infallible and inerrant. People have always tampered with scripture because it is the foundation of any religion, and in order to sway the religion you have to modify the scripture people hold to. This was done in Old Testament times, as well as the early days of Christianity, and it is done today. Only a prophet of God can be commissioned to make revisions in the Bible. So many copies of New Testament texts exist it is impossible to determine how the Bible should read, as a result we have many translations of the Bible, and we find the only way to make true corrections is through prophecy and revelation.

There'd be no point in learning Greek to study the original texts since there are 5,600 New Testament texts, plus 10,000 written in Latin and 500 in other languages, and no two are alike. The oldest known copy of the New Testament is only a small fragment that dates back to the 2nd century. There are probably 300,000 differences between the texts. Scholars have found that the scribes who wrote the texts were often bad spellers, forgetful in word placement, and sometimes left out complete pages. Since the 18th century, scholars have employed many techniques to reconstruct the recension of the text to determine their possible original writing, but no resounding conclusions have come forward. Efforts to cross-refer the texts have been made in hopes to create a more accurate Bible but the final results are based mostly on personal preference, which is usually based on tradition.

As a result there are currently about 30 versions of the Holy Bible written in English and when we examine the different versions we see they are targeted for specific audiences. Some are translated word for word, some from thought to thought, and some are combinations of both. The King James Version tells of the Prophet Elijah hearing a *still small voice (1 Kings 19:12,)* but the New American Standard Bible calls it the *sound of a gentle blowing.* In secular Christianity revelation from God or promptings of the Holy Ghost are not recognized. The KJV claims importance on *faith, hope and charity (1 Cor. 13:13,)* emphasizing the need for charity. Nearly every other version of the Bible replaces the word "charity" with "love," because charity is an outward service that closely resembles good works, where love can be a feeling of endearment. And the Weymouth New Testament completely leaves out the mention of the third heaven in *2 Cor. 12:2.* For huge changes, compare the Book of Psalms KJV to the other English versions, or go to a non-denominational Church where they have a Psalter on hand, they are practically different books. There are so many people tampering with the Bible, none of them are commissioned by God to make those changes, and they can't all be inspired by the same spirit. Just as the present day Bible is modified to suit audiences and issues of the day, we can also suppose ancient scriptures were modified in their times, people sometimes assume that the original Hebrew and Greek texts remained unchanged from the time they were originally penned until they were translated. But we see prophets of old constantly trying to correct people's principles and practices, which were according to the written records of their time. Thanks to modern revelation we can see how much of the Hebrew and Greek texts were changed before they even got to the hands of their translators.

Joseph Smith began making revisions and corrections in the Bible and restored the true meanings to many of the verses, passages and chapters of both the Old and New Testaments. He is harshly criticized for making those modifications as people quote *If any man shall add unto these things, God shall add unto him the plagues that are written in this book. (Revelation 22:18,)* This is the argument against new and modern scripture and revising the Bible. Funny, similar passages are found in *Deuteronomy 4:2* and *12:32* that would eliminate 2/3 of the entire Bible, and they ignore the fact that people are continuously modifying the Bible today. The difference is that Joseph Smith was commissioned by God to make changes in the Bible according to the Spirit of Prophecy, the same spirit the original texts were penned by *(Jer. 36:32.)* We know that those things revealed to mankind can only be understood through revelation and that most of Christianity and Judaism don't believe in revelation. Unfortunately, Joseph Smith was killed before he could finish making all the necessary corrections, and the General Authorities to date have not deemed it necessary to replace the KJV as of yet *(D&C 42:15,)* but we can be sure that when the time comes those corrections will be completed. Of all the versions, we feel the KJV offers the most correct meanings and the most powerful testimonies of the Gospel. When people ask if we believe in the Bible, this is the one we're referring to, and we tend to assume it's the one they are referring to as well.

Someday the President of our Church will receive the commandment from on High to start making corrections in the Bible once again, then we will have that sacred text in its fullest, and the sealed portion of the Book of Mormon will be translated as well. A prophet of God must do the corrections of the Bible through the spirit of prophecy and revelation. There are too many copied texts to get an accurate translation from, the efforts have produced numerous versions of the Bible that are no more correct than another, and a prophet of God did make some corrections that vastly expanded our understanding of that great text.

Some might feel it is disrespectful to point out the flaws of the Bible, but to me it is more like seeing the wounds and scars on a great warrior who has seen many battles and campaigns, to recognize what it has undergone for the sake of others. Its testimony shines through in spite of its abuse, even as much as the Savior himself. Some make the Bible as much a myth as their gods are, ignoring the truths about both, and never understanding either. *(2 Cor. 2:17.)* With these things in mind, we still hold to the simple statement; *We believe the Bible to be the word of God as far as it is translated correctly. (Article of Faith No. 8)*

Chapter 9: Authority of the Bible

There are some simple rules for playing music, usually for those who are subject to simple and stupid mistakes, which applies to all of uss. For instance, the right note played at the wrong time is a wrong note. The wrong note play at the right time is still a wrong note. But a wrong note played with AUTHORITY! That's interpretation. When you have played an entire piece without a single recognizable note, but with AUTHORITY! That's artistic expression. Oh, yeah. Stop when everyone else stops and don't play any leftover notes.

Biblical authority refers to the writings of the Bible being authoritative over human belief and conduct and its accuracy in matters of history and science. Biblical authority is a theology developed in the 1970's and 80's when questions of principles, historical events, and scientific facts were scrutinized and challenged. Scholars determined that if anything but pure inerrancy or infallibility were taught about the Bible all Christianity would fail almost immediately. We know that authority from God does not come from the Bible, it comes from God. Let's see how Biblical authority is defined and explained, why Latter-day Saints do not accept these terms, and how we can accept the Bible as being true but not infallible.

Biblical authority includes issues of biblical inerrancy, infallibility, interpretation, criticism and Christian law. Biblical inerrancy takes the position that scholars are able to produce scripture near as possible to the original authored texts that can be confidently claimed to be the authoritative word of God. Two terms are often used; inerrancy—to mean there are no errors, and infallibility—to mean there can be no errors. These imply that the very nature of inspiration renders the Bible infallible and cannot deceive us, and is inerrant because it is not false, mistaken or defective. *Sola Scruptura* suggests that the Bible alone contains all knowledge necessary for salvation and holiness and demands that only those doctrines are to be admitted or confessed that are found using valid logical deduction or reasoning from scripture. Every single statement of the Bible calls for instant and unqualified acceptance. Every command of the Bible is a directive of God and therefore requires full agreement. Every promise of the Bible calls for unshakable trust in its fulfillment. Every command demands willing observance. Under these pretenses the Bible is self-authenticating, is clear to the rational reader, is its own interpreter, and is sufficient of its self to be the final authority of all Christian doctrine.

As Latter-day Saints we do not hold the Bible to be the final authority on all things spiritual or temporal. We believe God the Father is the final authority who gave His authority to Jesus Christ who in turn gave authority to men to act in his name, also known as Priesthood authority. We do believe the Bible to be the written records and testimonies of ancient prophets useful in teaching and instructing the principles of the Gospel, and the scriptures are records, histories and commandments of God given to mankind. However, the Gospel is an eternal principle that exists with God and cannot be preserved in the written word, while scriptures bear record of the Gospel, the Gospel exists throughout the Priesthood and those who have the Gift of the Holy Ghost, unifying God and man *(John 17:17-23.)* Through the years the Gospel has been reduced to the stories of Jesus, or the *synoptic gospels,* and the message of the Atonement, but we know that the fullness of the Gospel includes Priesthood authority and all things necessary to save men in the Highest Heavens. Because we believe in modern day prophets who receive modern revelation, it is impossible for us to believe the Bible contains all that God wants us to know, *We believe all that God has revealed, all that He does now reveal, and we believe that He will yet reveal many great and important things pertain-*

ing to the Kingdom of God. (Joseph Smith, 9ᵗʰ Article of Faith.) We do not believe the Bible to be inerrant or infallible since it has passed through the grubby paws of mere, mortal men for thousands of years. We don't believe that anyone is authorized to translate, edit, or modify scripture except a prophet who is commissioned to do so through the gift of translation *(D&C 45:60-61.)* To date we feel the King James Version of the Holy Bible is the most accurate English Bible and hold to it as a Standard Work to be included with other scriptures that help clarify its teachings. When we say we believe in the Bible, we do not mean we believe it is inerrant or infallible or the final authority for doctrine, we mean we believe in the principles of the Gospel found in the Bible. Those who believe in the principles of the Gospel will also believe in The Book of Mormon, The Doctrine and Covenants, The Pearl of Great Price, and other literature produced by the General authorities of the Church of Jesus Christ of Latter-day Saints.

We believe so much more than what is taught in the Bible. We are impressed by how much ancient prophets knew and understood, but often didn't tell or their writings were edited, yet some things slip through and we recognize them. We don't claim any scripture to be without error, ancient or modern, in fact, we believe there are as many things to create doubt in the scriptures as there are to create faith. The First Commandment; *Thou shalt have no other gods before me (Ex. 20:3)* implies that nobody or nothing has authority over Him. Of the things I have afore mentioned, individually they are almost harmless, but collectively the seem like idolatry. Our Heavenly Father wants us to be dependent on Him for the knowledge we receive. So we study and we apply the teachings in our lives, and we pray to know the truth of the things we learn, and the Holy Ghost manifests that truth to us. This is how weak and simple people, who are not well educated or eloquent speakers, can have testimonies that cause lions to fear. This is how early Apostles went from confused and timid followers to stalwart religious leaders. This is how the mysteries of God are made known beyond what is written in the scriptures and this is how ancient peoples had such perfect knowledge the Heavens could not be withheld from them.

I personally find it questionable when so many rely on deductive reasoning to exhume doctrine from scripture when the Bible clearly says *For the wisdom of the world is foolishness before God (1 Cor. 3:19.)* Dead Reckoning is not a principle of the Gospel, but revelation is, and that is how true doctrine is established. Authority to preach the Gospel, perform ordinances, and organize the Church does not come from the Bible, it comes from God the Father given to Jesus Christ and passed down through His prophets. We can see how evolution of theology drives people to the printed page, we can see how our Heavenly Father reproaches it, and we can see how truth can be known in spite of the tainted works of man.

Our fellow ministers of different denominations struggle with the same problems in society as we do. It isn't easy for them or their followers. They work diligently to teach people by the best means they have and they do remarkable work. The Bible is a good foundation to base their conduct on and by no means should they be discouraged from being good Christians. These people have a genuine love for others, they are taught to be genuine by their ministers, and they are taught to be so from the Bible.

Chapter 10: Righteousness: Imputed, Infused, and Free Agency

I saw the most impressive sight this morning while hauling a load of water to Ten Sleep. The snow covered Big Horn Mountains were over cast by thick clouds, and the rising sun lit up the undersides of those magnificent clouds reflecting back and forth from the mountains, the whole skyline took the most ethereal orange glow I ever saw. It lasted about twenty minutes and I didn't have my camera, dang it. I hear people talk of the cityscapes of New York and Chicago with their high rise buildings, but I find nothing manmade as magnificent as the wonders of nature.

The traditions of Christianity tend to vary on righteousness. Every major religion in the world believes in righteousness or the actions by which a person is judged by and justified in the eyes of God. The word appears more than 500 times in the Old Testament and 200 times in the New and is occasionally translated as *rightways.* Righteousness is our conduct in accordance with the laws and ordinances of the Gospel. The majority of Christians believe righteousness is either imputed or infused from God, where we believe righteousness is based on our free agency, and directed by divine assistance.

The difference between imputed and infused righteousness depends on whether righteousness is a status or a quality of religious or moral perfection. Imputed righteousness is the righteousness of God credited towards man for his faithfulness (passive,) infused righteousness is the righteousness from God in the sense of merit reward (active.) To impute is to attribute righteousness to a person vicariously, as derived from God. To infuse is to permeate with righteousness to alter life for the better. Imputed and infused righteousness rely on the notion that righteousness is strictly alien, or based on God's actions, and nothing humans can do will ever be acceptable to God, and righteousness is a gift from God that can in nowise be deserved. It is assumed that mankind is completely unable to achieve any amount of righteousness of his own efforts; therefore it must be given in some way by God, because God is the only one truly righteous. It has been said that there are two kinds of righteousness, the one without us by imputation, and the one within us through faith, charity and other Christian virtues by infusion.

The explanations are as numerous as the arguments for and against; it's a dizzying circle of tail chasers. In truth, righteousness is the quality of living resulting from obedience to the laws and ordinances of the Gospel. Righteousness is not imputed, infused, imparted, bled off, or intravenously injected. Righteousness is purely our efforts to live by gospel standards. No person can live wholly righteously, but we can attain enough righteousness to be counted among the Lord's own, and it is a means of spiritual progression. Those who lived worthy to come to this world also try to live the standards set for this world so we can be worthy receive higher rewards in the next. If we were not able to attain righteousness to salvation then certainly the Prophet Elijah wouldn't have been taken into heaven having never tasted death, Abraham and Job would never have been considered perfect men, and it would have been pointless for Jesus to command us to be perfect *(Matt. 5:48.)* Free agency is a term used almost exclusively by our Church. It is the right to choose between good and evil and to act for ourselves, and because we are able to choose, we are responsible for our actions. As we choose to obey our Heavenly Father's commandments we grow in character, strength and wisdom, we grow in faith, and we find it easier to make right choices. Of all those who insist that God is in control, it would be true to say that nothing can frustrate God's plans, but it would be wrong to say He is a tyrannical dictator who forces or coerces people. God may take a person's life for one reason or another, but He will not take away their agency. He allowed both Adolph Hitler and Mohandas K. Ghandi to make the choices in their lives, and each secured their places in the eternities by their actions, and the same is for us. Every person who has walked the earth (with their mental faculties intact,) even Jesus Christ, has had the choices between good and evil. Many will say that Jesus Christ could not have sinned and was beyond temptation, but upon reading His life's story we see He was tempted around every corner, even to the point Satan made personal efforts, and Jesus decisively and deliberately paid them no heed.

Many would say we simply cannot make those choices on our own, we don't have the knowledge or wisdom to do so, and only God can make those judgment calls. But we can make wise choices because our Heavenly Father gives us a hand, He gives us many hands; the scriptures to help teach us about the principles of the Gospel and many things pertaining to the Kingdom of Heaven, living prophets who receive revelation to instruct us on matters of the day, and the Holy Ghost to help us make decision in our everyday lives. When we attend our Church meetings we learn from the scriptures and from each other how to make better decisions. When we accept callings and magnify those callings we learn responsibility, consideration, time management, and resourcefulness. When we are asked to teach a lesson or give a talk we learn more in-depth the subject we are teaching through study and research and we learn to overcome many fears of being in front of people. When we share our testimonies we learn to express our feelings in the face of possible criticism. We learn courage through obedience and the weak are made strong. There are angels just beyond the veil who can help. All we have to do is to ask for it. It's how we learn.

It might seem that manifestations of the Holy Ghost might be a form of imputation or infusion, but not so, those manifestations are the results of correct choices. Inspiration from the Holy Ghost comes when we pray for guidance before we make our choices. Righteousness is the lifestyle molded from making choices based on the principles and ordinances of the Gospel. Many would say that it is a gift from God that is imputed or infused to change our lives, we say we are given commandments, direction, and freedom of choice, and our Heavenly Father has provided ways we can make correct choices in our lives.

Heavenly Father has laid the ground work for our roots, He has given us the standards of righteousness we should live by, and it is up to us to live up to those standards. We will be judged by the decisions we make and the actions we follow through on. Jesus Christ was the only man to lead a sin free life and showed us what was possible, we know that He was saved in the Kingdom of Heaven, so the only way we can be certain of salvation is to lead a Christ-like life. We must pattern our lives after His, follow His commandments, do the work He would have us do, and endure to the ends as He did. He was the living example of what righteousness was.

Chapter 11: The Need for Grace

Oil field work is always a dirty job. Everyone is always dirty and grungy, we take a shower every night and do it again the next day, and some guys who are away from home (most all of them) don't even bother for a few days. You want to stay upwind of them when talking because they get a little wiffy on the lee side. There's very few women working the oil fields and there's very few women protesting it, I don't think it's the kind of work women covet, and we don't find any aged or handicapped people out here, either. It's funny how people raise such a stink over equal employment opportunities, but I'm a healthy, white male who can't get a job at Walmart. We all have our places, some people raise a stink just to show the world who can stink the most, so we just stay upwind of them.

This is another age-old dispute, whether we are saved by grace or by works. Grace is an excellence or power granted by God. It is agreed upon by all Christians that salvation comes to us through grace from God, for Protestants salvation is by grace alone and Catholics hold to salvation through grace combined with righteous works. It is by the grace of God that we have our very existence but we know also that grace is added upon according to righteousness. People began depending on righteous works through Jewish history, and that same dependency developed in the Catholic Church which Protestant reformers tried to break away from, but we know that salvation is conditional requiring us to take responsibility.

I call this an age-old dispute because it goes back much farther than our Church, farther back than the reformation, and farther back than the Catholics. The Apostle Paul talked about this problem in his epistle to the Romans. He knew as well as we do that ancient Israel followed the gospel of Jesus Christ and baptized with authority *(1 Cor. 10:3.)* He also knew they fell out the true practices and rebelled *(vs 5.)* We see many times how the Lord sent prophets to try to restore righteousness among the Israelites, and each time they insisted redefining their laws and practices in ways unacceptable to the Lord, eventually they strayed so far from the Gospel and became so dependent on their laws they became convinced (and still are) that the righteousness of their actions were the keys to salvation. So when their Savior did come they didn't feel they needed a redeemer. Paul addressed this problem in Romans 3 and emphasized the need for God's redeeming grace through the Atonement.

After the apostles were killed off, the Christian Church was left to deal with its affairs not by revelation but by the intuitions of schooled ecclesiastic leaders. When Emperor Constantine took the leadership of the Church he had his counsels wrote creeds which dictated who and what they were to worship, and organized the priesthood in his own hierarchy system. *Sacerdotalism* was not a new thing in the Catholic Church, it was a true Priesthood order set forth by the Savior *(1 Peter 2:9)* to include Apostles, Prophets, Evangelists and Teachers *(Eph. 4:11,)* Seventy *(Luke 10:1,)* High Priests *(Heb. 5:10,)* Bishops *(Titus 1:7,)* Elders *(Acts 14:23,)* Priests *(Luke 1:8,)* and deacons *(1 Tim. 3:8,)* all of which are offices held in our Church today. The Catholic Church also introduced ordinances such as infant baptism, absolution, indulgences, penance for sin, and veneration of relics. The Church denied the common people the opportunities for education and kept religious material from them. And probably the most abusive practice the Church actively engaged in was the inquisitions (or the fighting of heretics) in which people were tortured or publicly executed if guilty of heresy.

In 1517 a salesman, Johann Tetzel, was collecting indulgences when a young priest, Martin Luther, decided he had enough. He couldn't understand why the Church was taking collections to redeem souls when Jesus Christ did that on the cross. He wrote out his famous *Ninety-Five Theses,* pointing out the erroneous practices of the Church, and tacked it to the door of the Castle Church in Wittenberg, Germany. Naturally he was excommunicated and condemned an outlaw. He taught that salvation did not come by works, but strictly by grace through faith in Jesus Christ and His atoning blood, and he opposed sacerdotalism considering all baptized Christians to be a holy priesthood. He also taught that the Bible was the only source of divinely revealed knowledge. Luther completed a German translation of the Bible by 1534 and published it for the common people but was criticized for trying to manipulate the Bible to his own teachings. He also had issues with the books of Esther, Hebrews, James, Jude and Revelations. He couldn't see how Revelations could possibly have been inspired by the Holy Spirit, and he viewed James as the "epistle of straw," since he could see very little that pointed to Christ and His saving work. He felt to exclude these books completely from his Bible but decided to just shove them to the end. Martin Luther is a credit to Christendom; he helped establish religious diversity and freedom, and gave the Bible to the people, but he did not receive revelation to establish true doctrine and correct means of worship, he could only make do with what he had.

So this is the separation of Grace and Works, the very same problem with early Christians and the ancient Jews repeated all over again through Catholics and Protestants. We are, in fact, given gifts from God freely without any merits on our own parts. But salvation is not one of them. Salvation is conditional, meaning we have responsibility in it. So what are the gifts of God given to us *without* merit? Life, both in spirit and the natural, a beautiful world upon which we can reside, the knowledge of good and evil which initiated procreation, the Atonement of Jesus Christ for the redemption of mankind, the resurrection of all mankind, the gift of eternal life, and the degrees of glory which we will be judged worthy to receive. All these things are given to mankind whether they are righteous or wicked or whether they deserve any goodness from God. The Atonement of Jesus Christ is one of the graces of God, the pivotal point for salvation and given for the benefit of all mankind, but it is not the only requirement for salvation. In order to receive the highest rewards we must accept that atonement and strive to live righteously according to the commandments of God. Salvation requires us to do our part *(Phil. 2:12-13)* in which we receive grace upon grace *(John 1:16,)* or that which we have will be added upon according to our righteousness. When we make covenants with God, He makes specific promises concerning our salvation, and we agree to live up to the terms and conditions that He has set. *I, the Lord, am bound when ye do what I say; but when ye do not what I say, ye have no promise (D&C 82:10.)* If we don't live up to our end of the deal then God owes us nothing. He has already done for us more than we could ever be worthy of, but He wants more from us and He wants to give us more, and to receive more we have to strive for more. If we want the prize then we have to run the race, it doesn't mean we have to come in first place or that we even have to start at the same time, but we do have to finish it. The onlookers from the sidelines do not get the prize. The critics don't get the prize. The refreshment stand, the beer booth, and not even the chase car get the prize.

All too often it seems that grace is a substitute for responsibility, either we cannot do anything to merit salvation or that we don't have to do anything, implying that ineptitude or laziness is A-Okay. Through the grace of God we all can have everything needed for eternal life but salvation in the highest degree is conditional on our parts. Traditions of the Jews have been set strongly on good works, and early Catholicism corrupted many righteous works spawning the Protestant reformation, but we know that the greatest rewards of God are conditional and not given to irresponsible slackers.

Our brothers in the Christian ministries labor diligently to bring people closer to God through the proclamation of the

Gospel. Catholic and Protestant traditions have been established by some of the greatest minds in history and often sealed by their blood and trials. To examine their teachings and consider them is to pay respect to and honor their devotion and earnestness. Some might find their eternal rewards grossly disappointing, but most of them studied, proclaimed, and lived with all the sincerity and heart to the knowledge they had, well deserving of the rewards God would amply give them.

Chapter 12: The Need for Works

Tonight I stand next to the guard shack overlooking a barren oil well. They spent the last four months fracing (Induced Hydraulic Fracturing,) I got to help haul water in and the waste water out, and now I've been demoted to guard shack duty. They didn't get all the oil they were hoping for and now they're tearing down the equipment and moving out. They finished taking the frac tanks out and the vent pipe down, now they just have to take down a few storage tanks and dis-assemble the pump unit, and after this week-end they'll take the guard shack. I guess I better look for other work.

In the previous chapter I talked about the separation of grace and works. Protestant reformers separated themselves from the practices of the earlier church and settled on the scriptural accounts that justified their grace based ideals. This has become the tradition of Protestants. As Latter-day Saints, we believe the need for good works is every bit as important as the need for Grace. We can see how ideals became traditions, how New Testament accounts were directed, and the fact that all true religion has been established through covenants of righteousness.

In my research on Christianity I have found some common messages concerning the righteous works of mankind; we cannot keep all the commandments, we cannot earn merit for salvation, and we can only be justified by faith. The most common teachings of Protestant churches are; confessing the divinity of the Lord Jesus Christ; justification by faith alone; that good works are the products of faith but not necessary for salvation; and that people are predestined to salvation by the election of grace. Each of these concepts is only briefly mentioned in the Bible, so their vagueness has allowed these concepts to develop into erroneous theories, and these theories over time have become traditions. Orthodox means to adhere to accepted norms in religion, usually the creeds of the early church, but those who teach outside the accepted norms are considered radicals, heretics, schismatics, and cults. We can see Protestant churches falling into the same habits as the Catholic Church they were separating from. Because of the discredit of righteous works many of the ordinances of the Gospel have been done away with and often those still professing to believe in them feel they are only symbols of faithfulness rather than necessity for salvation. Ministers often refer to this passage; *For by grace are ye saved through faith; and that not of yourselves: it is the gift of God: not of works, lest any man should boast. (Eph. 2:8-9)* This is not a counsel for men not to do good works, but a counsel to humility, to remember that it is through the works of Jesus Christ in which these people were transformed into Saints. Emphasis on the need of grace in the Bible is aimed at Jews converting to Christianity or Gentiles raised in Jewish communities. Most of the Christians already understood the need for works and so there is essentially one epistle dedicated to that cause.

What we find between the Apostles Paul and James is not a dispute on justification, but two Apostles addressing two audiences on two points of the same Gospel. Paul addressed the Jews on Grace and James addressed the Christians on righteous works. Paul also taught the importance of good works to the early Christians *(Gal. 6:7-10)* and to the Christians in Philippi he counseled to *work out your own salvation with fear and trembling (Phil. 2:12)* making no reference to grace except in salutation. Each of the epistles of the Apostles are written to counsel the conduct of Christians except Paul's epistle to the Romans, which is regarded as the most defined concerning the graces of God and the Law of Justification, and nearly all Protestant Christians hold it as the core of their beliefs. But Christians today are not Jews who need counseling in accepting the graces of God for salvation but are Christians who need counseling on the importance of doing good works, just as the early Apostles counseled the early Christians. Some ministers are precisely as Paul described; *They profess that they know God; but in works they deny him, being abominable, and disobedient, and unto every good work reprobate. (Titus 1:16)*

We know that salvation comes through both grace and righteousness; *We believe that through the Atonement of Christ, all mankind may be saved, by obedience to the laws and ordinances of the gospel (Joseph Smith, Article of Faith No. 3.)* Salvation is a two part effort, grace from God and the righteousness of His people, agreements are made to secure that salvation provided we live up to those agreements, also known as covenants. Anywhere you find revealed religion you will find the people making covenants with the Lord. *(Gen. 6:18 Adam; 9:12 Noah; 17:11-14 Abraham; Ex. 6:4, 31:16, Num. 25:13, Lev. 26:42, Deut. 4:13 Moses; 1 Sam. 18:3 Jonathan and David; 2 Kings 23:3 Manasseh King of Judah; Ps. 50:3, Isaiah 59:21, 61:8, Jer. 31:31, 50:5 the Lord with His people; Mal. 3:7-12 the covenant of tithing, Matt. 26:28 Jesus and the New Testament, Heb. 8:6 Jesus the Mediator, 13:20 blood of the everlasting covenant, John 6:54 Jesus administers the sacrament.)* I rattled off this list from the Bible specifically to show that covenants have been an important part of true worship throughout the Old and New Testaments. At present, the only ones who enter into covenants with the Lord are members of the Church of Jesus Christ of Latterday Saints. Where there are covenants there are also ordinances, physical actions that represent spiritual promises, certain rites and ceremonies specifically known through revelation. Many of these ordinances are baptism, laying on of hands for the gift of the Holy Ghost, sacrament, receiving Priesthood authority and callings, marriage (more specifically Celestial marriage,) temple initiatory and endowments, sealing to spouse and children, and doing all the same work vicariously for the dead. Many people out there make pledges of commitment to the Lord and call them covenants, but if there are no ordinances performed by those with Priesthood authority, they haven't made covenants.

We can't accept a fragmented Gospel torn between orthodoxy and reformation. We know that it is the combination of grace from God with the righteousness of mankind that provides salvation in the Highest Heaven. The ideals of justification and grace can be supported in the Bible, but we can see that scriptures are directed towards audiences who are not always Christian, and we can see how true righteous works are established through covenants.

I think people hope they won't be rewarded or punished for their actions but hope their actions will be defined by motive, that way they can better justify themselves rather than better behave. The separation of grace and works came about because of the corruption of good works; much of that corruption came about by the effort to make Christianity spread through the world, and the reformers made the effort to end the corruption. I believe that orthodox and Protestant leaders have had the best of intentions in developing the theologies to better mankind. I believe they have always tried to prepare people for higher rewards in this world and the next. The good they do for their people and society is a blessing to all of us.

Chapter 13: The Law of Justification

Writing is a gift, there is no doubt, and it seems to me that those with the greatest gifts are very spiritual people who draw their creativity from the greatest Creator of all. It wasn't long ago that I did something I knew was wrong, not a really bad thing, certainly not worth mentioning here, but something I knew did not impress the Lord. That wonderful gift was taken away. For two solid days I couldn't pound out a solitary word in this book, I completely lost connection with any of the work I already laid down and nary had a thought concerning it come to my mind, to say the least I felt devastated. After the first night I felt the sorrow and regret of my action and prayed very sincerely for forgiveness. After the second night I concluded the Lord would help when He decided was good. Early on the third day I went to the temple, as I sat in the endowment room my soul and my mind began to fill, and before I could leave the parking lot I fired up my laptop and let the words gush. I was elated, I couldn't type fast enough, and I spent more time correcting my spelling than actually writing. I cursed my mortality. Perhaps my actions were not as severe as losing 116 pages of translated manuscript, and perhaps I didn't feel my soul racked to be doomed in hell, but I certainly understand what Brother Joseph felt when the Lord took his gift of translation away. You might make other mistakes in the future but you'll never do that one again.

Justification seems to be a heated debate in the Christian world. It's mostly debated according to the books of James and Romans, whether a person is justified by their works or by the grace of God through the Atonement of Jesus Christ, some believing that earning merit for salvation diminishes Jesus Christ's work. Latter-day Saints know it is by the power of the Holy Ghost in which we are justified. The traditional views of justification are at the foundation of this conflict, but a true understanding of this doctrine clears the issue, and we see how it applies to temple work.

The secular Christian view of justification, simply put, is God's pardoning sinners through their faith. As all humanity is fallen and sinful, they fall under the curse of God and are incapable of saving themselves from justice and punishment, but under the Atonement of Jesus Christ sinners are given judicial pardon or justification. *Sola fide* (faith alone,) the Protestant view following Martin Luther's descriptions, proposes that faith in Christ is sufficient for sinners to be accepted by God and supply them with trust, gratitude and love toward God from which good works are produced. Good works are the products of faith but are not required for salvation, because a person cannot gain merit for salvation through works, salvation comes strictly through faith in the Atonement of Jesus Christ. Justification is an event through which the Atonement makes it possible for people to be reconciled before God and cannot be lost.

While Protestant justification is passive, Catholic justification is active, that salvation comes by both the grace of God and the righteous acts of people, that there is a mutual effort and if people do not prove their faithfulness the Atonement will not justify them and they will be punished for sin. It is by obedience to the laws and ordinances that satisfy the divine laws and merit eternal life, salvation is earned in cooperation with the Atonement, so a person can be saved. Justification is a process, starting with the first justification through baptism, struggling through life to maintain righteousness, and concluding with the end justification at death. With this notion, justification can be lost through mortal sin.

So, every point has a side and every side has a point, but that's beside the point. As Latter-day Saints we do believe in justification. *And we know that justification through the grace of our Lord and Savior Jesus Christ is just and true; (D&C 20:30.)* We know that justification is essential to our salvation but it's not what people think. It has nothing to do with God pardoning sinners through their faith or works. Justification is how we know where we stand in the eyes of God *(Rom 5:1-2.)* It is any righteous act justified, ratified, or approved of by the Holy Ghost *(1 Cor. 6:11.)* This is how we know that the things we do in faith are actually accepted by our Heavenly Father, whether it be changing the tire for an old lady or administering an ordinance in the temple, we can know we are meeting with approval from on High.

We know that mankind is saved by both grace and works, and upon grace we can know in full confidence that God has done his part, but it is our part that is questionable. Since we know that we have to do all things in faith *(Rom. 14:23)* then the only way we can know that our actions are acceptable is if they are justified by the Holy Ghost. All covenants, contracts, bonds, obligations, oaths, vows, performances, connections, associations, or expectations must be entered into and sealed by the power of the Holy Ghost in order for them to hold any merit in the Kingdom of Heaven *(Matt. 18:18)* This law is the provision that no unholy act can be considered binding or effective in the eternities. Baptism by other churches are not performed by faith according the proper Priesthood authority and therefore cannot be justified by the Holy Ghost, and therefore cannot be made binding, not any more than going for a swim in the pool. Civil marriages may be legally binding according to the laws of the land, but are not justified by the Holy Ghost, so that marriage covenant ends at death.

This more particularly applies to the temple work we do for the dead. First, we don't always know if that person is worthy to receive those ordinances, and second, we don't know if that person is willing to accept them. But those things really aren't for us to determine, we are not the judges, just the workers. So we do the work anyway, we are not condemned for performing ordinances for a person who by no means deserves them, and this again is where the justification through the Holy Ghost comes in. If that person is worthy and does accept the covenants and ordinances then it will be ratified by the Holy Ghost and the work is made sure. If it isn't then there is nothing binding in it, that person is no better off than if their name was never entered into the records. Again, that's not for us to decide.

In my studies I haven't found anything in traditional Christianity so far off from revealed doctrine as the Law of Justification. To say we're not on the same page would be an understatement; we're not even in the same library. It is through the power of the Holy Ghost that makes the things we do binding in Heaven. It is the traditions of Catholics and Protestants that have brought conflict to the books of Romans and James, but we know what true Justification is, and we know how it applies to both the living and the dead.

Through the power of the Holy Ghost we can know the truth of all things *(John 16:13)* and through that same power we can know that our actions and our lives are in accordance to His will, and those treasures we lay up in heaven, the acts of our faith, are accepted by the Lord and made manifest through the Holy Ghost. I don't know how others can know they are saved, by grace or by works or by confessing the name of Christ or whatever, but I know that by the power of the Holy Ghost we can know where we stand in the eyes of God and we can work our way back to Him. The Holy Ghost guides us and justifies us.

Chapter 14: The Law of Sanctification

I went for a short drive in the Jeep today and saw some of the fresh powder laid this morning, the area looked like a winter wonder land. Just the other day it was warm and sunny out, for once I didn't have to plug the Jeep in, and I changed out the starter and went for a relaxing drive in the mountains. I remember a few years ago it snowed eighteen inches this time of year. Right now I can see a storm coming through the canyon. I think the weather report said there will be a torrential monsoon tomorrow. Yep, looks like spring is settled in.

Unlike justification, sanctification hasn't been precisely defined as orthodox or reformed doctrine. Nearly all Christian churches believe in sanctification but there are many interpretations, their beliefs differ based on whether sanctification is a process or a one-time experience, or if entire sanctification is possible in this life. Sanctification is to make holy, set apart or consecrate, and to make free of sin. How a person is sanctified depends greatly on their belief structures, we know that it deals mostly with our own conduct, and that not only is it possible but we've been commanded to be perfect.

Some claim that sanctification is based on works while justification is only by faith while others claim it cannot be attained by any works based process but only through the works and powers of the divine. Eastern Orthodoxy teaches that sanctification is the doctrine of theosis where humans take on divine properties by taking on Christ's divine nature. Roman Catholics believe that for the individual, sanctification is a close union with God resulting in moral perfection and that it is regulated by standards such as the doctrine of the love of suffering, and that suffering purifies a person's love of God. Lutherans teach that sanctification comes by the Holy Spirit through the preached word of God while Methodists teach *entire sanctification* by which God's sanctifying grace cleanses people from the corrupting influence of original sin and is a life-long process of healing a person's sin-distorted perspective and way of life. Some claim sanctification is a definitive act of God's grace at the time of conversion while others believe it is that plus a progressive act afterwards.

Sanctification is a purification process that prepares a person spiritually to ultimately return to our Heavenly Father *(Heb. 2:11.)* It works with faith, repentance and forgiveness, all being principles of the Gospel. For a person to be baptized and become a member of the Church of Jesus Christ of Latter-day Saints they must live up to the basic standards of the Church. If they are not living up to Church standards they must go through a repentance process that brings them up to snuff. The most common habits people have to break are smoking, drinking and extra-marital relations. When they are baptized they are washed clean of all sins, as the repentance beforehand prepared them for baptism but did not cleanse them from sin. Afterwards most people continue in life and are subject to temptation and are very capable of sin. The law of sanctification allows a person to continue learning and repenting of sin, and justified by the Holy Ghost, without having to be re-baptized every time they do something wrong. In time they become worthy to receive temple ordinances and then continue to grow spiritually until they are as perfect in the eyes of God as they can be in this life. Some grow and mature more than others, the more so the better here and the more advantageous in the next world, but the Atonement of Jesus Christ makes up for anything a person couldn't correct in this life.

In comparison to other Christian faiths, we have to say that sanctification is a life-long process involving strict obedience to the laws and ordinances of the Gospel, and that entire sanctification or perfection is attainable in this world. We know this by the accounts given of Noah and Job. We know that Jesus Christ was not the only perfect man to walk the earth, but he was the only man to lead a completely sinless life, other men have attained perfection but through sanctification as I described above. In the Bible we are commanded to be perfect *(Matt. 5:48)* as Abraham was *(Gen. 17:1)* and the ancient Israelites were *(Deut. 18:13.)* The trials of life are testing points to see if we will rise above adversity and turn to God for help and strive with greater determination to do better. Sanctification allows us to reach that measure the Lord has set for us. Many of the things taught by other Churches tend to be fragmented and are not entirely accurate. Sanctification is not a magical or mythical state, but a real and practical means of improvement as directed by our Savior. Yet it is every bit as grand and important as the most profound visions of the greatest prophets.

I think one problem with sanctification is that people get it all mixed up with justification. With the correct understanding of justification we can clearly see the importance of sanctification and what it means to be set apart and made holy. Theology has produced many views on sanctification, but we know that we must make the effort to become a holy people, and that we have been commanded to be perfect even as Abraham was.

Christian ministers can't deny that sanctification is important, not if they believe the Bible as they say they do, but to expound on sanctification risks taking importance away from the traditional teachings of justification. It becomes an issue between grace and works. Furthermore, guidelines for conduct, or principles, have to be established which allow people to become sanctified through, and those principles can only be revealed from on High. They would have to practically devise a whole new religion based on those principles. No, wait. That's us.

Chapter 15: The Law of Election

On August 20, 2011 I had the fine opportunity to witness the grand opening of the Heart Mountain Interpretive Learning Center dedicated to the memory of those Japanese Americans who were confined in ten relocation centers during WWII. Since I was on the film crew for the daughter of one of the internees I got to listen to the interviews of those who were sent there. It was really very touching to hear their stories and testimonies, some were still embittered from the ordeal, but most continued to lead happy lives and had fond memories of the camp. I told some of my fellow college students and some friends of the experience and they seemed so complacent, as if imprisoning our fellow Americans for no real reason was not important in our history, and some actually justified the action. Apathy is easy when you are so far removed from the problem.

The election of Grace is not so much a widely promoted concern because of its negative implications. While this theology claims that some people in this world are predestined for salvation and that their actions will have no consequence in their eternal rewards it also considers people to be predestined for hell on the same conditions. Such being the case it would be possible for Adolf Hitler to be saved in the Kingdom of Heaven while Mahatma Gandhi roasted in hell. The theological tradition of the law of Election could never allow God to be just and merciful as we know that He is. Protestant reformation addressed the issue of the elect and has since produced diverse conclusions, while modern day revelation has produced a new element, and we can see more clearly God's intentions for the progress of mankind through election.

Undeniably, scriptures speak of some specific cases of election, or predestination. It is the call of individuals to office or honor in a religion, and it is agreed that Abraham, Jacob, Moses, Saul, David, Solomon and the Apostles of Jesus Christ were predestined for their places in life and have secured their salvation. There is also the election of a nation, or the covenant people of the Lord which would be the true church or religion of God, as were the ancient Hebrews and the early Saints. Election is often associated with John Calvin during the Protestant reformation. It is at the good pleasure of God and His claimed right to save as He sees fit, and it is not a condition of faithfulness or of repentance, as those are the products of God's regenerative work. Predestination is often considered a *paradox of free will,* where God's almighty power is incompatible with human free will and is often associated with other forms of determination such as destiny, fate and doom. Christians following the teachings of John Calvin typically accept that God alone decides the eternal destinations of each person without regard to their choices so that their actions or beliefs are in accordance with God's will. It is also being taught that God has two wills; a sovereign will and a moral will, the sovereign will dictating people's eternal rewards and the moral will revealed to mankind. Teachings of predestination often bring up questions on the omniscience of God as to whether He is eternal or atemporal, or free from the limitations of time or causality, and that an all-knowing god must be able to foresee all future events and predetermine people's destiny.

One crucial element is missing in the theory of election; the pre-existence. All of the references of God knowing people before they were born does not pertain to God's foreknowledge of future events, as tradition would hold, but actually knowing those people as spirits living with our Heavenly Father before we came to mortality *(Jer. 1:5, Eph. 1:4.)* Through modern revelation we know that all things were created in spirit before the natural, that we went through a period of progression and schooling, and that we were given responsibilities and agency to conform to laws *(Abraham 3:26.)* Those who became great and noble ones were foreordained to perform great missions for the Lord in this life. A good number of us were not quite so valiant and some not very good at all, but all those who are here managed to qualify for a mortal body and have potential to return to God, while a third of the host of heavens entered open rebellion with Satan and were cast out from the presence of God and were denied the privilege of mortality *(Jude 1:6.)* A veil of darkness was placed over our eyes so we could not remember what we were like so everyone had a fair chance and full free agency to choose good or evil. And a plan of salvation was implemented which included repentance, sanctification, and the Atonement to aid our spiritual growth and progress.

By far the most complex system of people coming into this world is through the election of Grace, or the assigning of people to come into the world at correct times to do the Lord's work when it would be most effective, and this involves lineage. For example, the most righteous of prophets in the Old Testament came through a line of righteous people unbroken from Abraham to that prophet. Even Jesus Christ came from an unbroken line of righteousness directly from the House of David giving Him not only a spiritual heir to the Kingdom of Heaven but a temporal heir as literally the "King of the Jews." We know that many Latter-day Saints were reserved to come forth in the last days before the Second Coming because of their obedience in the pre-existence and their desire to help build the kingdom of God on earth with minimal, if scarcely perceptible, promptings from the Holy Ghost. But we also know that foreordination and election does not guarantee admittance to salvation, anyone who has come to this world (including Jesus Christ) has faced temptation and made their choices according to their knowledge and understanding, and we can see by the example of David that anyone can screw up. It is beyond our capacities to comprehend the design of God which brings us here at the right time through all the generations of mankind to be the unique individual doing his own small part to further the work of God, but we try our best to live up to the expectations we agreed to before we came here.

The election of Grace is not so unlike justification in which it is a true doctrine of God but has been horribly distorted through theology and tradition. These traditions making claim on God's sovereignty do not allow for His justice. The theories originating with John Calvin have developed into multiple conclusions, but with a proper understanding of the pre-existence, we can see how this true doctrine works through the universe to bring choice people into the world when they can be most effective.

I don't know how anyone can think they know the kingdom of Heaven without revelation. A friend of mine once said she couldn't understand why Joseph Smith did so much guess work. I didn't know how to respond at the time, but as I've done research for this book I can see nothing but guess work in the theologies that have evolved through the centuries, and each theologian laying claim to the mind and will of God as if it were his own.

Chapter 16: Sin

The last time I saw my beautiful aunt alive was two weeks before she passed away due to complications of old age. While I visited I reached down to pet her cat she had for several years. As I fondled the cat's ears and neck, I patted down its back and started scratching that itchy spot just above the hips, that place that drives cats crazy, and suddenly, as quickly as you could snap your fingers, the cat spat and lashed out with its claws. I had moved my hand just in time to miss the razor slashes. The cat glared at me as I pointed my finger and said, 'Hah! I know you.' Then I walked away. The first time I ever petted this cat I wasn't so quick, in fact, I found in most cats that if I just let my hand go limp they would cease their attacks and trot away. Not that time, my hand ended up scratched, chewed and mangled in ways I didn't think possible for a domestic animal. Nobody really understood why this gentle creature would snap and turn so violently on a loving hand. Many people refused any affection at all. But from that first encounter I learned to recognize the signs and if I just paid attention I could successfully pet this cat and avoid needing medical attention afterward. I never avoided the cat or refused it attention, I never punished it for its ill temperament, and I certainly never sought to antagonize him or make him afraid of me. I just made sure that my hand was clear immediately after he turned his ears back and spat. That was the nature of the beast.

A sin is a violation of known moral rules according to a religion. Violations of State and Federal laws constitute crimes and sometimes the two are intertwined, but many sins are not against the law. Sin isn't always just our actions but also our thoughts, feelings and internal motivations which might be considered immoral, selfish, shameful, harmful, or alienating. Sometimes we sin because of ignorance, sometimes because of weakness, and some-times out of defiant disobedience. We all sin for one reason or another and it's a broad enough category to cover everyone. Since there is such a broad range of people both good and bad, we have to look at the levels of severity of sin that would call all people to repentance.

I've had several people ask if I was a Mormon and if I felt drinking coffee was a sin. Reluctantly I've said yes because I know the next question to roll off their lips, *Do you think you'll go to hell for drinking coffee?* Incriminating questions are not meant to be fair. First, sin is all manner of wickedness or unrighteousness. *(Ps. 94:23, 1 John 5:17)* To be wicked is to be evil by nature, fierce and vicious, and to cause harm, distress or trouble. It is the outward and deliberate effort to hurt others in some manner; physically, emotionally, or mentally. Wickedness is the most basic and vile of sins, and the cruelest in severity, God will have no place for them in His kingdom. There is hardly any place for them in society and they end up spending their time on earth in jail. Since these are so cruel and vile they also require the greatest faith and repentance to overcome. Addictions can be counted with wickedness since peo-ple will rob, maim and lie to supply their dependencies (although not to be mistaken with chemical dependency.) Wickedness goes against the conscience, or the moral understanding between right and wrong, and anyone of rational thought is capable of following their conscience. So there is no excuse for wickedness. There is no admittance into the Church unless extensive repentance is done.

The second is to transgress the laws. *(1 John 3:4)* The laws of God are clearly stated in scripture with basic examples given. Living prophets can expound on those commandments so they are appropriate for the times and cultures. When we make cov-enants we are agreeing to abide by those very specific laws and when we break those laws we break our covenants. The saving grace of the Laws of God is; if you don't know the laws you are not held accountable, you simply cannot break a law you're not aware of. However, salvation comes through obedience to the laws and ordinances of the Gospel. So while you're not condemned for ignorance you're not saved, either. This notion causes much conflict for those believing strictly in a bilateral heaven/hell system. Teaching the Gospel is so vitally important so people can learn what is expected of them. Then it is those laws by which people will be judged by, to knowingly disobey is sin, and to not repent is destruction. Members who do not repent of these wrongs face reprimand from the Bishopric, dis-fellowship, and possibly excommunication.

The third is to know good and not do it. *(James 4:17.)* Where the commandments of God are generalized and basic, this notion is more specific to the person and their ability to use their own judgment, and is also more of a matter of conscience. This can range anywhere from good manners to humanitarian aid for victims of natural disasters. There may not be specific laws given on this topic but we have rational minds and we can often easily see what is needed of us. For example, if you are the first person at the scene of an accident and you know CPR, the right thing to do is administer help to the victim until help arrives. Prison guards are liable for the safety of the inmates they oversee, if they knowingly let an inmate suffer injury without rendering assistance or aid, they can be fired or sued for negligence. We are seldom bound by law to do good, but we are bound by conscience, and we'll be judged by that, too. We don't need every little detail of our actions spelled out for us, we're adults here, and the Lord expects us to take responsibility for our actions. Many of these things are not serious enough to be taken to the Bishop. Usually they just make you look stupid or lose some respect from your peers or family.

And finally, anything not done in faith is sin. *(Rom. 14:23.)* This operates in the finest details of our lives, our every action and decision pivots on this principle, and it's the polishing cloth that makes us shine. Sins of this nature are so negligible they're hardly recognizable as any actual wrong doing. For instance; me sitting and watching a movie instead of working on my next best seller, I know this is work I need to do, even though there is no pressing need or deadline. I know the Lord wants me to get to work and the devil would rather I veg-out. The time it takes to correct myself is almost as quick as the decision itself. This is being mindful to the Lord as He wants us to be, to consider our every action and determine if it is something He would have us do, if we're not sure then we pray about it, and the Lord wants us to always pray. *(Luke 21:36)* So whether I drink coffee or not is between my Bishop and me when I want my temple recommend renewed.

Sin is so much more than waywardness or basing your life on a lie. Sin is what separates man from God and repentance is the struggle to draw closer. Free agency allows us to make choices and we don't know all the facts behind each situation, so we're all subject to sin. Knowing the levels of severity in sin we can determine better where we stand with God and how we can improve.

Doing all things in faith is the perfecting of the Saints. This goes beyond the commandments or the conscience, or good manners; it becomes a quest for obedience. This is what allowed the entire city of Enoch to be translated *(Moses 7:9,)* this caused Abraham to offer his only child as a sacrifice to the Lord, this allowed Moses to lead the children of Israel out of Egypt, this is what caused Jesus Christ and the Apostles to suffer cruel deaths to demonstrate their faithfulness, this is what caused the early Christians to suffer death by lion's den rather than deny the Christ, and this is what allowed Joseph Smith to restore the Gospel of Jesus Christ. This is what caused Mormon pioneers to walk across the plains to make a burnt-up lake bed a home. To adhere to this rule allows for nothing less. It is in this manner the heavens are opened, the elements follow commands, and the veil of darkness is diminished. This is how we achieve perfect faith.

Chapter 17: Repentance

I e-mailed a Pastor friend of mine one time if he would tell me what repentance was, I mean I have learned about it in my own Church and felt very comfortable with its principles, but I wanted to hear what a Protestant reformed Baptist non-denominational Christian had to say. In response he asked why I was interested. So I told him I had heard many people talk about it and I wanted to know his personal views. He asked who had been talking about it. I said on the Internet, on the radio and on TV. He didn't answer back, and I don't know why, unless it's just a bit difficult to nail down as I have found out.

They say God hates sin but loves the sinner, or similarly said by St. Augustine of Hippo, but I disagree, I think God loves the repentant. Repentance is an important principle of the Gospel and every Christian religion places great emphasis on it. John the Baptist called people to repentance as did Jesus Christ when He began His ministry and each of the Apostles counseled people to repent. All Abrahamic religions teach the need for repentance in order to be joined with God. The call to repentance is an invitation for holiness. Repentance seems to take on a mythology all its own, yet we know the practical applications which help people draw closer to God, and we know that we are not predestined for sin just because we're human.

It surprises me just how vague repentance is in the Judaic-Christian world. John Calvin felt that repentance carried three attributes, first; that repentance was a true conversion of life from a serious fear of God, second; a mortification of the flesh and a change from the old man, and third; a vivification of the spirit (or to enliven, brighten or sharpen.) I heard a Pastor talk the other day say that you can tell a true Christian because of the light and liveliness in their eyes, where a non-believer is dead in the soul. Many Christians teach that repentance does not earn God's forgiveness from sin but they are called to repentance so they may feel their inability to do so and are thrown upon God to petition His grace in their hearts. God *grants* total repentance as each person responds to repentance in faith, as Jesus Christ suffered punishment for sin, and just like righteousness, repentance is imputed or infused. The same Gospel that calls for repentance also produces it. To Jews sincere repentance is equivalent to rebuilding the Temple, the restoration of the altar, and the offering of all sacrifices. Repentance is manifest through resisting temptations under similar conditions and is a prerequisite of atonement, or Yom Kippur. No one needs to worry of their sins since every penitent sinner is graciously received by God, even on their death bed, as it is never too late to repent.

Still, as long as we are human we are corruptible, tempted, and capable of sin, and therefore have cause for continuous repentance. As Latter-day Saints we know there is a process. Of the first two levels of sin I mentioned previously, these need to be addressed to the Bishop, he will council and walk a person through this process, of the other levels a person can rely on their own integrity to follow the process as applicable. *1) Recognize the sin (Luke 16:15;)* you can't fix the problem until you see it and confront it. *2) Feel sorrow for the sin (Isa. 57:15;)* regretting the action is the motivation for not doing it anymore. *3) Forsake the sin (Prov. 28:13;)* as Dieter F. Uchtdorf said, *Stop it. 4) Confess the sin (1 John 1:9;)* you have to confess all your sins to the Lord to be forgiven of them, and depending upon their severity they may need confessing to the Bishop so he can help correct the problem, or to the proper authorities so justice can be dealt or rehabilitation programs can be initiated. Repentance is about overcoming the problem by whatever means possible. *5) Make restitution (Ex. 22:5;)* if possible try to right the wrong. Apologize for hurt feelings, pay back money or return items if stolen, confess the truth if lies were told, restore a good name if you slandered it, etc. *6) Forgive others (Matt. 6:14-15;)* you cannot expect the Lord to forgive you if you cannot forgive people around you for having human weaknesses. This is a tough pill to swallow, but the Lord will not forgive unless your heart is completely purged of hate, bitterness, and bad feelings towards others. *7) Keep the commandments (Prov. 19:16, John 14:15;)* you know the rules so follow them, it's the least you can do, and if you can't do that then all of this is pointless. Jesus Christ suffered the pains of hell so we wouldn't have to, the conditions of forgiveness are based on our repentance so God can be merciful, if we do not repent then Christ's suffering was in vain and we will receive justice.

This sounds like a recovery program, and by all rights it is, a recovery from worldliness. To assume we can just change our minds about sin is about the same as changing our minds about having a broken leg, it's not practical nor is it effective. Repentance is a healing process; just like our bodies need a healing process our spirits need a process to overcome sin. We don't accept the concept of "Original Sin," *We believe men will be punished for their own sins and not for Adam's transgression. (Article of Faith No. 2)* We're not damned just because we're human, and our human condition does not predispose us for sin, as we see by the life of Jesus Christ. The lives of righteousness or sin are strictly of our choosing. We all make mistakes but it is up to us to learn from them and try to do better.

In a world of *turn or burn* salvation it seems repentance is more of a threat than an invitation. Repentance is a call to draw closer to God, not an effort to kick us away from the fire. A certain amount of vagueness is required in Christianity to make it acceptable, but we can see how plain and practical the Lord has made repentance, and we can see that our human condition allows us the choice to sin or repent.

To overcome sin requires faith in Jesus Christ. By definition faith is the trust, hope and belief in a person, concept or entity.

Faith in Christianity is based on the work and teachings of Jesus Christ and declares its distinction not by its faith, but by the object of its faith. Strangely, evangelical views on faith are equivalent to their views on repentance, extremely limited. Granted, they place great emphasis on the need for faith, as they do with the need for repentance, but very little practical knowledge is out there.

Chapter 18: Faith

I went on a hunting trip not long ago, my friends took me along, and they knew the area better than me. We took a topographical map along so we'd know the terrain and where the roads were. I've hunted since I was a kid so I know the routine; guns, ammo, dress in layers, energy snacks, knives & hatchets, get up early and hike around a lot, make a clean shot, and get up to your elbows in entrails. Deer and elk are elusive critters, you have to know them pretty well to hunt them, and hitting them with cars isn't really hunting. It's not a matter of trying to think like an animal, where they would hide to get away from hunters, but knowing what they need. Food, water and bedding; get that figured out and you'll find their hang-outs. Then you look for trails, tracks, fresh scat, rubs and scrapes. Then get ready, even if you don't see the critters, you can bet they're not far away. Funny I should use hunting as an analogy for faith, but it is written; *Now faith is the substance of things hoped for, the evidence of things not seen. (Heb. 11:1.)*

Faith is not the most controversial issue in religion, its meaning may vary among the world religions, but in Christianity there's not that much dispute. Faith is the confidence or trust a person places in an entity, usually a deity of sorts. Depending on the religion, faith can be monotheistic (single god,) polytheistic (many gods,) henotheistic (many gods but worshiping one,) or kathenotheistic (worshiping different gods at different times or seasons.) Monolatrism is kind of like henotheism except it recognizes the possibility of other gods and dedicates worship to only one while henotheism allows other people to worship their own gods believing they'll get the same results. Clever, eh? Faith in Jesus Christ is the first principle of the Gospel and a spiritual gift necessary for salvation. The meaning of faith differs slightly from the denominations, but we can see through the aid of a true prophet how true faith is demonstrated, and we can receive all the Lord offers us for happiness in this world and the next.

People have definitions for faith that share great similarity. Christianity declares that it is not distinguished by its faith (religion) but by the object of its faith (Jesus Christ.) Faith is an act of trust or reliance that leads to an active life aligned with the ideals and examples of Jesus Christ. Faith is built on understanding found in the community of believers, the scriptures and traditions of Christianity, and the personal experiences of the believer. Faith is belief in what is true and comprising two elements; being convinced of the truth and embracing the truth. Faith is good only when it is placed in truth and when placed in falsehoods can lead to eternal doom. Understanding the word of God and religiously obeying is the most direct to spiritual perfection and people must accept the whole Bible to be whole Christians. True faith requires people believe all that God has said about Himself and of people, that until they believe just how bad they really are, they can never truly accept the graces of God. Objectively, faith stands for the sum of truths revealed by God in scripture and tradition presented in creeds, subjectively, faith stands for the habit or virtue by which people hold to those truths.

But without faith it is impossible to please him: for he that cometh to God must believe that he is, and that he is a rewarder of them that diligently seek him. (Heb. 11:6) We know that only through faith in Jesus Christ can man be saved in the highest heaven, and certainly, not being saved in the highest heaven does not please God. In 1833, Joseph Smith began the School of the Prophets as special training for leaders of the Church. In his lectures he talked about three things necessary to exercise faith in God unto life and salvation. *1) The idea He actually exists.* It is the simple notion that you can't have faith in something you don't believe in. A certain amount of education is required about God and sometimes a person has to take a leap of faith, to try it and see what happens; we do it all the time for cheaper thrills. The only means by which we can know of God's existence is through the power of the Holy Ghost, a manifestation of truth, being a revelation acquired through a desire to believe and asking in faith. *2) The correct idea of His character, perfection and attributes.* Of His character we learn of His personal traits and moral qualities, those things which make Him anthropomorphic, or having human qualities. By understanding God we understand ourselves, the universe around us, and the wiles of Satan. We understand why we are *a little lower than the angels (Ps. 8:4-5, Heb. 2:6-7.)* We understand how we can be made perfect, like unto Him *(Matt. 4:48,)* and we learn the standards of righteousness. We can understand how we were made in His image *(Gen. 1:26-27, Abraham 4:27.)* Of His perfection we can agree with Aristotle in his definitions; that which is complete and contains all requisite parts, that which is good and nothing of the kind could be better, and that which has attained its purpose. More than anything it is a state of completeness. Through the Atonement of Jesus Christ, the covenants we make in the temple and repentance we can live up to the standards set before us. Of His attributes, or aspects which define Him they can be described in negative theology; He cannot lie, He cannot be in two places at once, and He is no respecter of persons. Or he can be described in positive theology; He is all powerful, all knowing, and His influence is over all things. *3) An actual knowledge that the course of life which we are pursuing is according to His will.* Where there is great faith there is also great doubt *(Ex. 4:10.)* The only way we can do the Lord's will is if we are worthy and capable to perform the acts required of us, it is through revelation that we can know we have been forgiven of sin and can move on to do the Lord's work, and it is through revelation that we know the work we are to do and that it is done correctly.

From these things we see that faith is a reciprocating altruism, an active effort initiated by us and rewarded by the Lord thus increasing our faith. *(Luke 17:5)* Faith is a principle of action and power that motivates our lives and each day we act on things we hope for even though we don't fully know the end result. Through faith and repentance we make the Atonement fully effective in our lives. We place our faith in Jesus Christ to become His obedient disciples in hopes that our Heavenly Father will forgive our sins and prepare us to return to Him. Our Heavenly Father is the only one who has full faith in Himself, Jesus Christ placed his faith in God the Father, and we place our faith in Jesus Christ. Miracles are brought about by faith, angels appear, and spiritual gifts are given. Everything our Heavenly Father does for us, outside those graces already mentioned, is initiated by us through faith. Even to have our prayers answered requires us to pray first. We have to draw a response from God through faith, so we have to call upon him in righteousness, and then we can reap the benefits of an all-powerful God.

All true religion has always been centered in Jesus Christ. Faith in Jesus Christ is the most important principle of the Gospel. Through time many views on faith have surfaced, but we know through a living prophet what is required in true faith, and we can know the benefits of exercising true faith.

We place our faith in Jesus Christ to help us return to the presence of our heavenly father. In Old Testament times people placed faith in Jesus Christ that He would someday fulfill His part of redemption, to suffer for the sins of mankind and to die on the cross, or all their efforts to lead righteous lives would have been in vain. Now we have the atonement fulfilled, we have to act in faith to lead lives worthy of that great sacrifice, so we can be counted among His own.

Chapter 19: The Atonement

All my life, as far back as I can remember, I've known of the existence of God. Undoubtedly being raised in the Church has formed and framed my views on religion, so I can understand my friends in other religions who hold to their traditions, and I try not to be too critical because they hold to those beliefs rather than convert to the restored Gospel. Everyone boldly claims to cleave to the truth of the Gospel in spite of the varying teachings. So a question arises, how does a person know truth? It's a question similar to Pontius Pilate's. We see bumper stickers that say *Jesus is the answer.* But anyone who has a simple answer is a damned liar and they haven't even explored the concept of truth. It's a haunting question that looks over our shoulders and questions the things we think we know, kind of like this stupid grammar checker. We can know truth like we know music. Regardless if people have been schooled in music or not they can tell what music is and appreciate good music. Most people can't tune an instrument by ear but they sure can tell when it's out of tune, and nobody really knows why. Our Heavenly Father has provided ways we can know eternal truths and how to recognized them. Those who don't know truth don't know who to trust. Truth leads to understanding and where there is understanding there is forgiveness.

The Atonement of Jesus Christ is the central issue of all Christianity. Of the western religions, Christianity is the only that places importance in the Atonement, as Judaism and Islam consider it irrelevant or unnecessary in the spiritual progress of mankind. It is strictly through the Atonement that God can be just and merciful upon His people. Christian theology has produced several theories on the Atonement, but we have to understand how the Atonement has redeemed mankind from the Fall of Adam and how it allows us to live righteously according to our Heavenly Father's plan.

Through the history of Christianity theologians have created four main theories on the Atonement. First, the *ransom theory;* teaches that Christ died as a ransom, supposedly paid to Satan, to claim the souls of humanity. Second, the *satisfaction theory;* Christ suffered as a substitute for mankind through his infinite merit and satisfied the demands of God's honor. Third, the *penal substitution theory;* Christ was punished in the place of sinners and satisfied the demands of justice so God could forgive sins. Fourth, the *moral influence theory;* the purpose and work of Jesus Christ were to bring positive moral changes to mankind through his martyrdom and resurrection. Each of these theories was developed through time and cultural changes. More recent concepts that I've personally heard are; that all mankind is redeemed from the Fall of Adam to be saved in the Kingdom of Heaven; that all those who profess the name of Jesus Christ will be saved; that all sin is made legal or righteous through the Atonement; that only those who have given their hearts and their lives to Jesus Christ will be saved; that all those whom Jesus Christ paid the ransom for cannot be lost again; that those who accept the Atonement will no longer have the desire to sin; and that people are guaranteed salvation upon accepting the Atonement in their lives. Some of these have elements of truth, some do not.

The Fall of Adam produced two kinds of death; spiritual and temporal. Spiritual death is to be cast out of the presence of the Lord and die according to righteousness and spirituality. Temporal death is the physical separation of spirit from body. The Atonement of Jesus Christ overcame both of these problems. Through his suffering in the Garden of Gethsemane Jesus paid the price for sin by which all those who would repent could be forgiven, and therefore be allowed to return to the presence of our Heavenly Father *(Luke 22:44.)* Through Christ's death and resurrection he permitted that all those who have died may be resurrected and receive immortality *(Matt. 27:52-53, Rev. 20:6.)* In this way Jesus overcame death and sin. Without the Atonement, the first judgment upon mankind would have remained indefinite and mankind could rise no more. It is through the Atonement that God can be just and merciful; justice can be issued according to sins which have not been repented of, nullifying the effects of the Atonement; and mercy according to the sins which have been repented of since Christ already paid the price of sin. The only way God can be just and merciful is if salvation is conditional upon the conduct of His people. The Atonement of Christ and the repentance of man must work together for the same goal.

The Atonement also allows people to live up to the commandment, *Be perfect, be of good comfort, be of one mind, live in peace. (2 Cor. 13:11)* We know there are two kinds of perfection; finite and infinite. Finite perfection is the ability for mere, mortal men to be complete in all the ordinances required for salvation and to follow all of the commandments in perfect righteousness. Infinite perfection comes after the resurrection when the corruptible takes on incorruptibility, when we are made physically perfect and are given all the rewards in heaven that have been promised, and we can reside in the presence of our Heavenly Father once again *(Rev. 21:7.)* Were it not for the Atonement, finite perfection could never be achieved and nobody could ever be worthy to receive salvation, except for Jesus who was the only man to walk the earth having never sinned. Yet, we know that Noah and Job were both men who walked perfectly in the eyes of God *(Gen. 6:9, Job 1:1,)* but their perfection was established through sanctification, or continuous repentance and overcoming sin. Without the Atonement, those sins they repented of could not have been forgiven, and their potential to walk perfectly in the eyes of God would have been destroyed. That was the point Paul was trying to make in his letter to the Romans *(Rom. 3:23-24.)*

Everything in Christianity rests on the Atonement of Jesus Christ. The Old Testament testifies of the coming of Christ and his Atonement, the New Testament testifies that he came and fulfilled his promise, and the Book of Mormon clarifies and re-affirms those testimonies. Justice and mercy are attributes of our Heavenly Father and it is only through the Atonement of Christ that God can be both. The traditions and cultures of Christianity have produced varying theories of the Atonement, but we must understand what the Atonement redeems mankind from and how it allows us to reach our fullest potential.

The entire Gospel of Jesus Christ is founded on his Atonement, there is scarcely a Christian faith that doesn't acknowledge this, and it is the concern for the human condition that so many theories are created. The principle is simple so that a little child can understand and yet its importance is profound to be the pivotal point of all Christianity. It is pivotal for the salvation of all mankind, and every mankind under every creation of our Savior, which are numberless.

Chapter 20: Absolute Truth

I sat in sacrament meeting today and one of the ward members gave a presentation on her violin. I noticed that she did the exact same thing as every other violinist I've ever seen; she tuned her violin first. I play guitar. It's necessary to tune a guitar because the fingerboard has frets and notes are established from a set point, if the guitar is out of tune the notes will be off. A violin doesn't have frets, so if it's out of tune, the musician can adjust her finger position to establish the correct notes. But in truth she really can't and still play the music, it takes too much effort and concentration to re-establish the correct tones, and the music is lost. From the time a violinist learns to play the instrument she learns that her fingers go to exacting places for the notes, and those positions become ingrained into her mind until they become a reaction instead of an action, she plays the music without thinking. The music which is written on the page is translated by the musician into a language that we understand, the emotions she puts into the work makes it an art form, and it becomes a voice that touches the listeners. The violin must be in tune or all her work is ruined.

Absolute truth is a concept being used more and more by evangelical ministers to support their beliefs in the Bible and in God. The concept started around the time of Plato who believed that absolute truth existed, but that truth on earth was merely a shadow of the absolute truths existing in the universe. They concluded that absolute truth itself could not be known. It is a philosophical principle adopted by many ministers to give their teachings substance. Absolute truth in Christianity rests on the notion that absolute laws are given by God and that this is how we know they are from God, and that God is the source of abso-

80

lute truth and to know God is to know absolute truth, but we find this philosophy is not part of the gospel or its eternal principles.

Being asked if we believe in absolute truth is like being asked if we believe in absolute music. It manifests itself in so many ways. Let's consider moral truths. On the issue of sexual morality Christianity requires it be between one man and one woman who are married. The worldly view is that it is acceptable for two or more adults to have consensual sex. The rapist might force himself onto his victim and say she deserved it. The child molester might manipulate his victims and say they wanted it. So we can see there is no absolute truth in morality because morality is a personal point of view. Turning to an outside source; it is assumed that the laws of God are standards that must be absolute. The most prominent three are #6) *Thou shalt not kill (Ex. 20:13.)* Applies to murder but does not apply to killing animals for food and raiment, killing in time of war or defense of home and family, or when God commands His people to utterly destroy *(Deut. 20:17.)* #7) *Thou shalt not commit adultery (v. 14.)* Meaning not to cheat on your spouse, but more universally accepted as not having sex with anyone outside the marriage covenant, but does allow for polygamy when the Lord so directs, and does not condemn victims of sexual assault. #8) *Thou shalt not steal (v. 15.)* Taking property that isn't rightfully yours, except in times of extreme need such as hunger and exposure. So we see that for every rule there are exceptions to the rule, and thus there is no absolute law. *(2 Cor. 3:6)*

Then there is the assumption that God is the absolute truth. He is the source of all truth, He is undefiled and pure, He is complete and perfect, and He has no limits or bounds. These are the definitions of the word *absolute* and can be applied to what we know about God. These can also be applied to any god of any religion, so the absolute part could be imaginary and not absolutely Christian. And the part about truth; corresponding to fact or reality, or a quality of being real or actual, then this rules out finding God through philosophy, science or mathematics. We can only know the existence of God through revelation, and a convincing testimony to me may not be convincing to someone else, so the knowledge of God cannot be absolute. Furthermore, the philosophy of absolute truth suggests that the only way an absolute truth can be known is through the affirmation of a negative contradiction. The phrase, *There is absolute truth,* cannot be proven as we have already shown it does not exist in morality, law, or the knowledge of God. So the negative contradiction would state, *There is no absolute truth,* and prove the positive by becoming the truth it denies. We can now say there is at least one absolute truth through contradiction. But this isn't possible either since a contradiction is a discrepancy or incompatibility, and is not truth at all. Now if you think that was fun, let's try this one; we cannot prove God exists as He can only be known through revelation, on the other hand we cannot prove God does not exist, as lack of evidence is not proof of non-existence. Scientific law says we cannot prove a negative until we first prove the positive, or in other words, we cannot prove something does not exist until we prove it once existed, like dinosaurs. So the negative contradiction cannot become the absolute truth it would deny. How are those for tail-chasers? But such are the ways of the world, if it is confusing it must be substantial.

Eternal truths are found in the Principles of the Gospel. We call them eternal for two reasons; first they pertain to and come from our Eternal Heavenly Father, and second they are truths that span the eternities, what is true today has always been true. The rules and regulations set for us not only have been applied through the history of all mankind, but for every other mankind on every other world God has ever created, which are without number. All the principles of the Gospel are found in the Bible but there is no listing of principles (unlike the Ten Commandments) which comes right out and says, *Behold, thus sayeth the Lord thy God, these are the principles of righteousness all y'all must show before me this day to enter the Kingdom of Heaven.* All the principles of the Gospel are found in the Book of Mormon, as well. So we can clearly see that those who truly believe in the Bible will also believe in the Book of Mormon.

Absolute truth is not an eternal truth as found in the principles of the Gospel, it is not revealed doctrine. Absolute truth is the philosophy of men ministers use to give the gospel substance since they teach against the principles of the gospel. It has become a substitute for principle. It is assumed that absolute truth can be found in absolute law given by God, and it is assumed that God can be known through absolute truth, but we know that eternal principles which are given to us through revelation do not include absolute truth.

As with all philosophy, absolute truth is a mind bender, one that comes to a ridiculous conclusion after there is nothing left to debate. Philosophy is an effort to establish truth through logic and reasoning and it is limited to the bounds of the human mind. The ways of God are not the ways of man and revealed doctrine often defies logic and reasoning, that's why we need the Holy Ghost to manifest the truth of them, and that's why we adhere to gospel concepts in spite of the absurdity. That's why we lose arguments all the time and still believe.

Chapter 21: Principles of the Gospel

It bothers me when people quote mindless clichés as though they were profound philosophy. Many times I've heard someone say a certain person would give the shirt right off their backs, yet I've never seen anyone ever ask for the shirt off someone's back. One man offered me a dip of chew knowing full well I wouldn't take it, said he was just trying to be friendly, like tossing a drowning man a glass of water. People say if you do what you love then you'll never work a day in your life. Hogwash! George Lucas and Stephen Speilburg both do what they love and have worked themselves into health problems. Tiger Woods works relentlessly to perfect his game so he can be better than the other golfers. Liberace practiced piano ten hours every day! Those who say that probably always had money and never worked for it.

The principles of the Gospel are taught in the Bible by Jesus Christ and the ancient Apostles, we recognize them because we also teach them, but most churches don't. Since most principles direct personal conduct they are often considered good works and therefore superfluous. To research each principle we find dozens of opinions, but to look for all the principles in group we only find references to The Church of Jesus Christ of Latter-day Saints. Just like all other points of the Gospel, the principles of the Gospel had to be restored to their fullest. As principle and doctrine are defined, we can see how many principles have been distorted, and we can see many false doctrines and principles taking their places.

Principles of the Gospel are not the same as doctrine. A principle is a fundamental, primary, or general law or truth from which others are derived; they are also personal bases of conduct or management. Principles of the Gospel are general overviews of eternal laws and ordinances necessary for salvation. Doctrines are policies, positions, and systems relating a particular subject or principle. The principle of baptism tells us that it is vitally important to salvation, so important that our Savior also had to undergo the ordinance, to fulfill all righteousness. The doctrine of baptism tells us who has authority to baptize, precisely how it should be done, the covenant made with the ordinance, and the prayer recited. Principles are the milk before the meat. When people accept the principles of the Gospel they will accept the doctrines that bring them eye to eye with God. Those enemies of the Church who do not teach or believe in the principles of the Gospel will make repeated attacks on the doctrines of the Church.

Some principles are universally accepted in Christianity, without argument; the origin and fall of man, the redemption of mankind through the Atonement of Jesus Christ, the judgment of the righteous and the wicked and their eternal rewards, faith in Jesus Christ as our redeemer, and repentance. But the doctrines on these principles tend to be vague and the different Churches have variations on the messages. Many principles are completely dismissed as being important to the salvation of mankind. *Baptism*, one of the most important ordinances of the Gospel, is often trivialized and taught that it is merely a display of faith, but not essential to salvation. *The laying on of hands for the Gift of the Holy Ghost* is utterly a foreign concept practiced only in our Church. *Free agency* is twisted to teach that once a person has been moved by the spirit they are no longer in control of their actions and that God is in control of all things. *Knowledge of the Holy Ghost* and his purpose in the trinity is either completely dismissed or distorted to imply him as no real being but only the influence of God, and his manifestations are ridiculed. *Modern day prophets* are completely denied. *Scriptures* are limited to the Bible in its various renditions. *The Atonement of Jesus Christ* is reduced to His dying on the cross and taking all of mankind's sins and nullifying them.

Priesthood authority and organization are either corrupted or completely eliminated. *Covenants*, if made, are simple promises of good conduct with no doctrine or ordinances to accompany them. *Gifts of the spirit* are half-heartedly believed, and are often fraudulent public demonstrations, like magic tricks. Responsibility for our actions and service to others is acceptable but not really required as Christ's atonement justifies all actions righteous or not, so *obedience to the laws and ordinances of the Gospel* is also not required. *The law of chastity* is being reformed continuously and is even being modified to allow homosexuality and same-sex marriage. Views on the *Second Coming* and the millennium have so many variations they become more like personal opinions rather than principles. And they often talk about the *final judgment* and eternal rewards as though they were the Judges of Israel to determine who goes to heaven and hell. These are not all the principles of the Gospel, but the ones most notably misunderstood or corrupted.

Without these true principles the practices become perverted and true doctrines rejected. When we think about the restoration we often consider the First Vision, the ministering of angels, the heavens being opened to revelation, and the restoration of Priesthood authority and keys. But it was the restoration of all things in the Gospel, as we can see that everything mankind has laid his grubby paws upon has been infected in some twisted way, it could never be reformed by man to be the same as set up by Jesus Christ and his apostles. Some of these false doctrines are immaculate conception, the advent of Jesus Christ, justification by faith alone, faith founded on reputable facts, authority by membership or belief alone, imputed and infused righteousness, allowable sin, the rapture, the law of the elect, the law of faith, the doctrine of union with Christ, covenant of Redemption, and the bilateral eternity (heaven or hell.) Man being created in the image of God no longer means in His likeness but to be a representation, manifestation or reflection of God. Even prayer is disputed as an effort to manipulate God to a person's beckoning and therefore taking divine powers on the self. Teaching beyond the Bible is a criticism used by ministers guilty of the exact same thing. Protestant reformers generally had the attitude that if it couldn't be done right, then not at all, and their principles were based on defiance of established doctrines rather than revelation. This continues today as the Restored Gospel grows in popularity throughout the world and people approach their ministers concerning these principles. Many of the concepts I just mentioned are recent developments in response to eternal truths. So the plain and precious things are taken away and replaced with cunning and crafty double talk.

It is no different than the ancient Israelites who continually strayed from true Gospel principles and devising their own theologies. We know the principles of the Gospel through revelation as part of the Restoration. Knowing what principles are helps to see how true principles have been compromised and false doctrines have replaced them.

The Bible contains the fullness of the gospel, everything we believe as Latter-day Saints can be found there, but not in full detail. What we find are often shadows or glimpses, sometimes just hints that to most people are not readily apparent, many things that don't hold enough relevance to conflict with traditions or important enough to be expounded or removed; things that are hidden from the insincere.

Chapter 22: The Rapture and the Resurrection

I sat in Priesthood meeting today and we discussed the signs of the Second Coming, an issue concerning the Rapture came up, and I was surprised at how little anyone knew about it. Our unfamiliarity with the Rapture comes from the fact we don't teach it. I have sought occasion to research the Rapture since I have several Baptist friends set on this principle and desire to know what Mormons think of it. I offered just a few things I had learned about the Rapture and the true doctrines of the First Resurrection and everyone seemed surprised, so I thought perhaps I should include an article concerning these things in this book.

Rapture holds that the righteous living will be caught up to meet Christ in the clouds during His second coming and will be taken away from this horrible world while the wicked shall be destroyed. Afterwards they will be brought back as resurrected beings to live on the earth in a state of paradise with Jesus Christ. The notion of being taken up to meet Christ is derived from the passage in *1 Thessalonians 4:17*, which does justify their belief, but we know that this is an error in translation. We know it will be the righteous dead who will be taken up in the *morning* of the First Resurrection. The theology of rapture is fairly simple, but modern day revelation sheds light on the issue, and we can see how the final events will play out.

Many who push the theory give it the most glorious imagery even though the word itself is taken from the Middle Latin *raptura,* to be caught up or taken away, but more specifically seizure, rape and kidnapping. The word "rapture" does not appear in the Bible or any modern scripture; it doesn't appear in any LDS teaching manuals or writings of our General Authorities, you have to look into other people's beliefs to know what the heck it's about. Such being the case we can know it is false doctrine, whether it is even doctrine depends on who you talk to, Catholics and Orthodox Christians do not accept it as gospel so it is strictly a Protestant concept. And not all Protestants adhere to it either; American Protestants formulated the concept early in the 1800's and it was popularized by John Nelson Darby and Edwin Irving. Rapture is coupled with another theory; the Tribulation. While all those righteous Christians who have ever lived are taken up to the clouds they will be looking down on an arena of gladiators and lions (my own analogy) as those left behind will face the horrors of their destruction. It is speculated to take as much as seven years to wipe out all the wicked. There are also three theories concerning the tribulation; that the rapture will happen just before the tribulation, or that the rapture will happen during the tribulation so many of the saints will experience some of it, or at the end of the tribulation. It is even considered that during the tribulation time the raptured saints will return and take part in the destruction.

New Testament scriptures are vague on the Second Coming. Those who already knew about it didn't need to expound on it, so much information has been lost, and that information also had to be restored. We know it is the righteous *dead* who will be taken up, those who have made Celestial covenants and have been blessed to come forward at that time to meet Christ at His coming, and possibly take part in the destruction of the wicked, and they will be appointed as kings and rulers on the earth through the millennium *(Rev. 6:20.)* We know that the righteous *living*, those living according the Celestial or a Terrestrial law, or those living the Gospel of Jesus Christ or the laws of their religion or land to the best of their abilities, will live out their natural lives under the jurisdiction and leadership of Jesus Christ. They will continue to raise families in righteousness. We can suppose this includes those righteous among the Christians, Jews, Muslims,

Hindu, Taoists, and Buddhists, and other righteous of the world. The earth will be restored to its Terrestrial or Eden-like state and the continents will be pushed together as they were in the beginning. The Jews will be restored as the Lord's covenant people and they will be the ecclesiastical leaders of God's Kingdom on earth in Jerusalem, while The Church of Jesus Christ of Latter-day Saints will become the political leaders in America or the New Jerusalem, and together they will lead the righteous people of the other world religions and teach the Gospel of Christ. As those people grow in righteousness and accept the covenants of God, temples will be built at a feverish rate and genealogical records will come forward to do the work for countless generations throughout the history of mankind, and as the names of ancestors have their temple work done those people will come forward in what is known as the *afternoon* of the First Resurrection. At the end of the thousand year reign the wicked will be brought forth in the Second Resurrection. That is how the millennium will proceed.

At the end of the millennium Satan will be loosed for a short time to tempt people once again *(Rev. 20:7-8,)* then the earth will die or fall to a state that can no longer sustain life, all those who lived on the earth and by this time had been resurrected will receive their rewards *(vs. 12-14.)* Then the earth will go through its resurrection process and become a Celestial world fit for those of the Celestial Kingdom to reside on *(Rev. 21:11.)* Those of lesser glory will go to planets appropriate to their glories and live out the eternities there. Jesus Christ and His worthy disciples will be here on earth and be visited by our Heavenly Father. Those of the Terrestrial Kingdom will live on a terrestrial world to be visited by Jesus Christ, and those of the Telestial on a different world to be visited by the Holy Ghost. Those sent to the outer darkness, or Hell, will not be visited by deity but will be tormented by Satan and his minions throughout eternity.

Just this morning I heard a pastor on the radio talk about how all the saints would be taken up and made perfect in an instant, all those truths pertaining to God would instantly be put into their minds, and they would receive a glory beyond their imaginations. It is the hope of many that the righteous Christian will be taken from this horrible world so they can do nothing else but bask in the glory of God, but we know that righteous dead will take up those positions next to Christ and the living will stay right here. The theology of Rapture is a fairly recent development, but restored information has enlightened the righteous, and we know what to expect for the next thousand years.

Now we're not really sure what the American Protestant Christians have planned after they are taken up in the Rapture, they may not have thought it out that much, but I understand that Rapture insurance is available just in case they're not taken up. No joke.

Chapter 23: False Prophets

It takes a prophet to know a prophet, and so I think to listen to a prophet talk about other prophets is a soul stirring experience, I love to listen to President Thomas S. Monson talk about the previous presidents that he personally knew. It's almost as if I knew those men myself, of whom I've never met and wish I did, maybe someday I will. When President Monson was first called as president I heard a few hardened Hinkley fans criticize our new president, saying that he was nothing more than a story teller and that's not what we need heading our Church, but I'm a story teller too, and I know that it is the stories of our lives and in our lives that help shape our lives. Story tellers know how to connect with their audiences. That's why movies and books are such huge industries. Throughout history story tellers have always been central figures right along with the medicine men. It is the story that helps teach us and strengthen our testimonies. A story teller is just what we need at the head of this Church and what a grand story teller he is.

There are 27 passages in the Old and New Testaments warning people against false prophets. Since the early days of the Catholic Church it was determined prophets no longer received revelation from on High and that bishops, elders, and deacons would use theology and apologetics to refute arguments and answer questions concerning the Church. It was the fear of being accused of false prophecy that caused the denial of living prophets. But we know and understand the need for true and living prophets today and throughout the history of mankind. We can see that false prophets are numbered among the religions and myths of the world, we can see through simple observation how a plethora of

Christian ministers can be counted among the false prophets, and we can know what true prophets are.

At present there are nearly twenty five religions throughout the world claiming prophets as their founders or leaders, at least eight historical figures not associated with a particular religion have been credited as being prophets, and thirteen popular world myths emphasize the use of prophets. Thirty four men and women have come forth in the last 2000 years claiming to be the returned Christ, seven have claimed to be Muslim equivalents, and seven have been a combination of Christian and Muslim messiahs. This makes true the prophecy of Jesus Christ, *For there shall arise false Christs, and false prophets, and shall show great signs and wonders; insomuch that, if it were possible, they shall deceive the very elect. (Matt. 24:24)* In general, a prophet is an individual claimed to have been contacted by the supernatural or the divine and commissioned to deliver that message to a society. Traditionally, prophets are regarded as having a role in society that promotes change due to their messages and actions. A common theory among Christians is that a true prophet is 100% accurate in predicting events and cannot contradict the Bible in any way, since it is the final authority in all things spiritual. Many Christians do not accept this standard as all the prophets of the Old and New Testaments have prophecies that are yet unfulfilled and many of their teachings do contradict each other, such as the books of Romans and James, which casts doubts as to whether the Apostles could be considered prophets. For some the days of prophets ended with the death of the Apostles while others make the cut-off line after Malachi, the last book of the Old Testament.

In truth you can't be a minister without being a prophet, *and that no man can say that Jesus is the Lord, but by the Holy Ghost. (1 Cor. 12:3)* A manifestation of the Holy Ghost is a revelation and one who receives revelation is a prophet. *(Rev. 19:10)* Those who claim that Jesus Christ is the Son of God yet deny the power of prophecy are bearing a false witness, or a testimony they don't actually have, and are themselves false ministers and prophets. False prophets are amok in the world even if they don't claim to be prophets. In days before Christ false prophets taught people to deny the Christ and his eventual coming, nowadays they might not deny the Christ but they deny everything else concerning him, namely; the responsibilities men have in Christ, minimizing or denying the principles of the Gospel, and they will either deny spiritual gifts (tongues, prophecy, revelation, visions, healing, etc.) or fake having those spiritual gifts. They will often claim to know when the Second Coming of Christ will be, or that they are the Savior, and claim to know things through divination that are not spiritually edifying. They will often talk of being true Christians while spreading hate and discontent, stirring up anger and pitting brother against brother, and neighbor against neighbor.

False prophets always rise up against true prophets. False prophets do not follow all the principles of the Gospel and are not above badgering, fault finding, and criticizing anyone they don't agree with even though they are repeatedly warned against slandering *(Ps. 101:5,)* backbiting *(Prov. 25:23,)* speaking evil *(Eph. 4:31,)* and begrudging neighbors *(James 5:9.)* False prophets always adhere to past traditions and the sayings of dead prophets *(John 8:39-42.)* They deny prophecy in these days but try to explain how prophecy was received of old. They accept no other scripture than the Bible claiming it to be the perfect manifestation of God's word and that it alone contains everything God wants people to know. Those who claim to be Christians and have the Bible follow suit with the Jews of Christ's time when they claimed to be the children of Abraham and had the Law of Moses. Furthermore, they either deny any kind of hierarchy of Priesthood structure or maintain one not organized by revelation. They deny the true nature of God based on falsified claims in the Bible that were altered to suit the traditions of the time. They emphasize the need for correct theology supposing the reasoning of man will create an understanding of God. They teach against good works even though those good works are the outward symbols which testify of a person's faith (*John 13:34-35.*) *Ye shall know them by their fruits* (*Matt. 7:16.*) An evil tree cannot bring forth good fruit.

True prophets do not speak in riddles or codes that need super computers to decipher, or in mysterious poems speaking of events that can only be recognized long afterwards, or in any matter concerning the Gospel that cannot be manifest by the Holy Ghost. For most people a certain amount of spiritual preparedness is required to fully understand prophets. True prophets testify of Christ and acknowledge his power and capabilities. They teach by the power of the Holy Ghost and teach others how to recognize and follow those same promptings. They know and understand the processes of revelation and teach people how to receive revelation for themselves and they realize that those things which have been revealed can only be understood through revelation. True prophets adhere to all the commandments of God and the principles of the Gospel. They realize the problems of people modifying, destroying or losing scriptures through time and must have modern revelations to clarify and understand ancient texts. They know that scriptures are most often records of prophets addressing issues of their day and know we need new revelations to address the issues of our day. True prophets receive revelation to help people prepare for future events, sometimes disasters, and help them prepare for the Second Coming. A true prophet carries authority given by God through proper channels and ordinances and carries the Keys of the Priesthood required for the governing use of that Priesthood. They know that scriptures are not the gospel but bear record of the gospel. True prophets are spiritual leaders for all people, not just a few select followers, but anyone that needs temporal or spiritual aid. A true prophet is a prophet to the world.

I mentioned that there were 27 passages warning people against false prophets, but there are also 29 cases of people rejecting true prophets because they didn't know the difference. We can't assume that because the Bible warns of false prophets that there will be *no* prophets and we certainly can't assume God no longer reveals His will because people quit listening. We know that true prophets are on the earth today. False prophets are everywhere we look these days, but we can know what false prophets are and how they work, and we can know this by knowing how true prophets work.

True prophets are necessary as mouth pieces for the Lord. It isn't because God can't talk to people, it's because most people are not ready to receive revelation, just like the ancient Israelites. When Moses called upon God on Mt. Sinai the Lord spoke to all the children of Israel, but they turned and ran in fear, then they told Moses that he should hear the Lord and tell them the word of God *(Ex. 20:18-19.)* You see, not everyone is worthy to hear the voice of God but everyone is worthy to hear the voice of a prophet.

Chapter 24: A Different Gospel

Consider the ladies. I can't help but admire them for their abilities to be kind and compassionate; it's their nature, something that men seem to have to learn. I suppose that is why the Priesthood is given to us, to learn compassion, and to be of service to others. Not once can we ever use the Priesthood for ourselves. Even Jesus Christ, the son of God with power in heaven and on earth, could not use His power to pull Himself off the cross. The chief priests and scribes were right when they said He could save others but could not save Himself *(Matt. 27:42.)* It seems so natural that women are in tune with the spirit and so responsive to it. I think Satan works hard on men because of that Priesthood authority, because the very heavens are opened through the Priesthood, and so he muddles our hearts and our minds. We seem so needful of those wonderful ladies to sustain and support us and keep us on the right track, everything always seems so clear to them, without question. Yep, I want to go to heaven because that's where all the hot chicks are.

A different gospel is a concept quickly spreading and being used against Mormons. It is the notion of being taught a different gospel as prescribed by the Apostle Paul in his epistle to the Galatians *(Gal. 1:8-9.)* There is no doubt that the Gospel of Jesus Christ as revealed to Joseph Smith is different than the Gospel reformed thousands of times since the death of the Apostles. Through the restoration of the fullness of the Gospel we can see how far secular Christianity has strayed. We can see how the gospel is regarded in a historical perspective, how far removed from true gospel teachings people have gone, and why it was so important that a full restoration was needed.

Catholic and Orthodox Christians hold to the notion that their version of the Gospel is unchanged from the days of Jesus Christ. But from the time of Constantine to the Protestant reformation we can see many vast changes in the Church that deviate from Gospel principles, the Dark Ages testify of this, from this we can clearly see their gospel is not the same as taught by the Apostle Paul. The efforts of the reformers was to return to genuine practices and principles as spelled out in the Bible, to get back to the original gospel, unfortunately far too much had been lost at that point. The gospel through time has been reduced to the story of Jesus Christ's ministry as found in the synoptic gospels of Mathew, Mark, and Luke. They are considered the source of many popular stories, parables, and sermons that are similar enough to be derived from a common source or borrowed content from each other. The principles of the gospel are not considered part of the redeeming good news to mankind. There is more focus on the origins of the synoptic gospels, their dating, locations, contents, their genre (if they were intended as novels, myths, history, or biographies,) and whether the book of John should even be included as canonized gospel. It is apparent that the four gospels were supplementary testimonies to teachings already circulated as Matthew addresses Jews, Mark and Luke address the gentiles, and John addresses Christians already converted. Unfortunately, the initial teachings of the gospel have been lost and we only have the supplemental testimonies, leaving the actual teachings of the gospel up for grabs, sort of a free-for-all. Yet people still think that the Gospel they believe is the same as taught by the early Apostles. There are so many Christian Churches; each different in name, organization and teaching because the details of how to organize a Church are not given in the Bible. They are the different gospels they preach against.

I mention from time to time the *free-for all* gospels. This is my own term I use to describe the varying gospels that teach that all things can be forgiven through grace; that by this grace all things are made lawful, and sins will not keep a person out of heaven. In these cases it is acceptable to live beyond the commandments, but with the knowledge of the Atonement, you simply wouldn't want to. They teach that the knowledge of sin becomes the desire for sin. Anything done on our part, the good works produced by faith, is taking credit for our salvation and denying the Atonement of Jesus Christ. With these things in mind anyone can be saved in the Kingdom of Heaven without concern for conduct, salvation itself is a gift from God through the Atonement of Jesus Christ, and it is literally "free for all." On the bathroom stall of a truck stop I saw this quatrain carved; *Sex is evil, sex is sin. Sin is forgiven so sex is in!* The free-for-all gospels would allow for this trash (apparently so did the truck stop manager.) These are doctrines of ignorance, they don't require a person to know God or the principles of the Gospel, and they don't require obedience or any amount of righteousness. It's the same principle Satan presented to Adam and Eve; open your mouth and close your eyes, and you will get a big surprise. This is all false doctrine. We have been warned about it numerous times in the Bible and we do not accept them.

Through time the Gospel had become so twisted and distorted that by the time Joseph Smith came along extensive restoration had to be done. The very first thing was the true nature of deity; Joseph Smith's first vision established that, then the restoration of Priesthood authority from those who held it last. Then the organization of the Church came forth bit by bit as the Church grew and changes have been made to suit the needs of worldwide expansion. Keys of the Priesthood were restored by their respective holders; these keys are the governing agents in how the Priesthood is administered and deal greatly in the ordinances, practices, and covenants Latter-day Saints commit to. And finally; revelations were given on how to prepare mankind for the Second Coming of Christ. As part of all this restoration, Joseph Smith was also commissioned to restore many passages in the Bible to their original content as penned by their authors. The Book of Genesis received the most correction, the first eight chapters were practically re-written, and so much correction was made that they became a new book of scripture, the *Book of Moses* in the Pearl of Great Price. Enough of the Book of Matthew was revised that it, too, was given a place in the Pearl of Great Price; other corrections have been included in the footnotes of the LDS versions of the Standard Works. These corrections help us to understand what our Savior wanted us to know. In the abundance of material we have through modern revelation and additional scripture, there are a number of important things we believe that are not written for public scrutiny, and the same was true during the times of the Apostles. Without those important teachings the gospel becomes a skeleton people can add material and make what they want from it.

This is the Gospel of Jesus Christ that was taught by the ancient prophets that became corrupt over time, that Jesus Christ Himself had to personally restore, and this is the same Gospel as taught by the New Testament apostles that they warned against perverting *(Gal. 1:7)* and also received through revelation *(vs. 12.)* The restored Gospel allows us to see how gospel theology, or the reasoning of man to understand God, has created evolved gospels so far removed from the original teachings they have become those different gospels. Historically the gospel is a group of stories, parables and sermons, and many people have stripped it of any real significance in life, but the restoration of its fullness has brought the Saints to a greater understanding of the Kingdom of Heaven.

This is the Gospel those same apostles were trying to protect. But if people don't know the laws, then they don't know the sins which transgress the laws, equally; if people don't know the true Gospel of Jesus Christ then they cannot know the corrupted ones, either.

Chapter 25: Heaven, Hell or Somewhere In Between

I took a chance the other day and bought a movie I'd never heard of, *King Rat* starring George Segal released in 1965, about a man who learns to lead a somewhat normal life in a Japanese POW camp. The images are wrenching as the producers afforded the true-to-life conditions of such a camp, the story was compelling as our fighting servicemen were left to degrade physically and mentally in conditions unthinkable with their struggles to hold to any sense of sanity or hope, and one man seems able to keep well groomed with neat clothes, fresh food, and even a Persian rug. He has men of different talents working for him, he has officers bribed, and he manages to manipulate the enemy guards. In a camp where everyone else is dressed in rags and eking out an existence, Corporal King lives like he's on welfare. Toward the end of the movie the war is over and the US Army brings in fresh supplies and restores order among the ranks. With all the men accounted for, updated on news, cleaned and clothed, and properly fed nutritious food, Corporal King finds he is no longer important. He becomes distant and falls into the shadows behind crowds of cheering men. In this world there have always been people proud of their pompous life styles and possessions but when all things are restored they too will become nobodies. *(Mark 10: 17-31)*

Previously I mentioned that there were degrees of severity of sin, such being the case there must also be degrees of glory to justify the lives of the righteous or wicked. If all life was so cut and dry, black and white, and good and evil, then the bilateral reward system might be effective. But there are too many variations of good and evil, a few people being perfectly evil and a few being perfectly righteous, and most of us are somewhere in between rocking the boat and making waves as we pass through the streams of life, flexing elbows with our neighbors, and spouting off at bad drivers as if we had Tourette syndrome. And you don't really know what a bad person is until you're related to one. The bilateral reward concept is strictly a manmade theology that does not allow God to be both just and merciful. The concepts of heaven and hell vary in the religions of the world, but the scriptures tell us of a temporary state for our spirits, and an eternal state after the final judgment in which justice is meted according to obedience.

Heaven is a common reference in religion, cosmology or metaphysics as a place for heavenly beings originating, enthroning, or inhabiting. It is often considered a higher place or state of being that people can either universally or conditionally access based on standards of goodness set forth by deity and the people's goodness, piety, faith, and right beliefs, and sometimes just by the *will of God.* Some hold to the theology of election in which those who were pre-selected will be given passage directly into heaven regardless of their actions or beliefs. If a person is not admitted to heaven they will go to hell. In many traditions, hell is a place of suffering and punishment in the afterlife. Some Christian ministers also teach of a temporary heaven and hell that spirits go to when people die and wait until the resurrection when final judgment will be passed and people receive their eternal rewards. Traditionally, Jews have taught of a place of temporary punishment, called purgatory, in which bad people go to receive justice in proportion to their offenses, not to last more than one year, and then are released in to heaven. Jesus Christ taught of the concept of hell being an unquenchable fire contrary to the belief of perdition and that it was a very real place and not just a state of mind.

The Jewish concept of purgatory is a shadow or hint of the Gospel principle taught in the Old Testament times. We know that there is a temporary holding place for spirits awaiting the resurrection *(Rev. 20:5,)* for those who were disobedient in this world that place is a prison *(Isaiah 24:22)* and for those who were righteous it is a paradise *(Luke 23:43,)* and a place where the departed can still receive the gospel of redemption *(John 5:25, 1 Peter 3:19, 4:6.)* Because of these passages we know that people can still accept the gospel after they are dead, and if they can accept the gospel of redemption, then they can also receive the ordinances of salvation *(D & C 127:5.)* The ancient Apostles knew of and practiced these ordinances for the dead *(1 Cor. 15:29.)* In the days after Christ's death and before His resurrection, we know He went among the dead to preach to them, and the vision given to President Joseph F. Smith helps us understand that Jesus organized and authorized the righteous spirits to go among the disobedient to preach to them and prepare them for the ordinances of salvation *(D & C 138.)* This process continues today as those authorized Priesthood holders and teachers who pass away from this world go immediately into the spirit world to begin their missionary work among the dead and prepare them for the ordinances we perform in the temples. As those who receive the glad message and accept the ordinances are released from that prison they will be allowed to be among the righteous in a state of peace and happiness *(Isaiah 61:1,)* and they will join the ranks of those who come forward in the First Resurrection *(Mark 10:31, Rev. 20:4.)* As they receive Priesthood authority vicariously they also become authorized ministers to aid in the teaching of the Gospel and prepare others for the same blessings. As missionary work goes among the nations of the Earth missionary work is at frenzy in the spirit world. We can't do temple work fast enough for those who are ready. Those who do not accept the gospel or its ordinances will wait in grief until the Second Resurrection, or the end of the millennium *(Rev. 20:5.)*

I have already talked about the resurrection and the millennial era, so I will move to the final judgment and eternal rewards. We know that after the millennium when all mankind has finished being resurrected, all those people will be judged according to their works *(Rev. 20:11-15,)* and those who were righteous will receive a heavenly reward while those who were wicked will receive damnation. And that's all fine for the most righteous and the most wicked, but what of those in between in which the bilateral kingdom doesn't account for? Many disputes have risen as to who will go to heaven and who will go to hell, and theology on the bilateral system all but eliminates people being judged by their works, but modern revelation has made allowances for everyone. The Kingdoms of Glory is not a new concept by modern day prophets, it was known and understood by the ancient Apostles, *There are also celestial bodies, and bodies terrestrial, (and bodies Telestial* as per JST): *but the glory of the celestial is one, and the glory of the terrestrial is another; (and the telestial, another* as per JST.) *There is one glory of the sun, and another glory of the moon, and another glory of the stars: for one star differeth from another star in glory. (1 Cor. 15:40-41)* The extremely brief and incomplete description of the degrees of glory allow for great speculation among the Christian denominations, but the Apostle Paul clearly claims to have known a man *caught up to the third heaven (2 Cor. 12:2.)* Modern day revelation has shed great light on this horribly abused principle. Only those who have received the ordinances of the temple and kept their covenants unto the end can receive the highest rewards in the Celestial Kingdom and receive all our Heavenly Father offers. *(D & C 131:1-4)* Those who have lead righteous lives according to the laws they have been given and to the best of their understanding of the gospel, but have denied the Celestial laws either in this world or the next, will be granted the Terrestrial Kingdom. *(D & C 76:71-79)* And those who have rejected all higher laws of righteousness, have been lead away by deceivers, have been victims of circumstance, have unremorsefully violated laws of the land, or have not overcome the temptations of the world, and those who have suffered the hell of spirit prison enough to be released at the end of the millennium, may receive the Telestial Kingdom. *(D &*

C 76-98) The glory received by each person in these kingdoms will be directly proportionate to their obedience to the laws of God and according to their works. *(Rev. 20:13)* But those who have been the sons of perdition and deliberately and knowingly have done the work of Satan, who were the deceivers who lead others away from God, who lead people into wickedness, the instigators of destruction, the tyrants who destroyed life without just cause, and those who fought against the laws of God, liberty, and justice, will receive an eternal hell. *(D & C 29:38, 2 Peter 2:4)* By the time of the final Judgment these people will have suffered the hell of the spirit prison for at least a thousand years, and some as much as the six millennia before, will receive their resurrection and be returned to their eternal anguish and be tormented by Satan without end.

This is the only way that God can be both just and merciful, meting rewards equivalent to their works, and giving everyone every possible opportunity they will accept. The bilateral system established by theology and proposed by much of the world religions cannot make allowances for wide range of goodness and badness among the people. The world has found countless ways to justify heaven and hell, but the scriptures teach that there is an intermediate spirit state, and an eternal state by which all will receive according to their obedience.

I find it comical sometimes. In order to get into the highest heaven a person must abide by the strictest standards of the Gospel, make covenants and receive ordinances, and endure faithfully throughout their lives. But you don't even have to believe in hell to go there.

Chapter 26: The Historical Facts

The Peregrine Falcon *(Falco Peregrinus)* is a majestic predatory bird found in nearly every continent in the world. It is known for its blazing 200 mph dives and its ability to snag other birds out of the sky. For 3,000 years this has been the primary bird used in the art of falconry; to hunt small game for sport. They have also been used to intercept homing pigeons during WWII and to deter birds around airports and prevent damage to aircraft. Due to its hunting and striking power it is often associated with aggression and martial prowess. In many cultures it has symbolized royalty and sovereignty. The World Center for Birds of Prey in Boise, Idaho, is known worldwide for its success in breeding peregrine falcons and releasing them into the wild, helping to remove them from the endangered species list, and also working with other birds of prey to help recover their populations. The main device on the back of the Idaho State quarter is the image of a peregrine falcon, which is not the State bird nor is found only in Idaho, but for those who keep insisting—*it's not a magpie!*

Anything that cannot be proven wrong isn't worth believing in. This is a scientific principle, any concept or theory that can't be falsified can't be factual. In reality there are too many variables in each situation to calculate and predict more than a controlled and limited outcome, so everything that can be proven right can also be proven wrong, and that is the substance of reality. But the lack of reality is the very strength of mythology, the fact that it cannot be proven wrong, therefore people feel confident in believing in it. Mystery holds weight. But true religion is founded on revelation. Theology often uses history to build its claims, but history is not an exact science, and scriptures are testimonies of events not necessarily written for historical accuracy.

I heard a fella a while back preaching on the radio and claimed that true religion was based on historical facts. And back before that I heard a man say that true religion was faith founded on reputable facts. I mentioned that in the late '70's the scientific and historical accuracy of the Bible was brought to question and religious leaders began pressing the issue of the inerrancy and infallibility of the Bible, and both of these gentlemen referred to the Bible for their historical facts. It seems religion is never beyond science, either religious leaders attempt to use scientific findings to help support their belief structures or scientists try to demonstrate how the miracles of God can be accomplished in a very realistic and explainable way. In recent years historians have been attempting to demonstrate how the events in the Bible may have been true and how the miracles written may have been possible. Their possible solutions to complicated situations or disasters are really quite impressive. But they've never explained how prophets of old were able to know beforehand the events that took place.

Historical facts are facts about the past. They help piece together the events of the past so we can understand better what happened. Historians try to learn why events happened, what caused them to happen, what effects the events had, and how those events were interpreted. This is why news or current events are not considered history, because not enough time has elapsed for people to analyze context, cause, and effect of events over time. The problem with history is that people of that time have no real idea how any particular event will effect society over time so they don't really know what information is most important to record, so a great deal of information is lost. So in order for historians to reconstruct what may have happened they compare stories from numerous sources, find common elements in the stories, and compare them to archeological findings, if possible. Unfortunately, history and archeology are not exact sciences, but then neither are geology and astrophysics. Come to think of it, none of the sciences are exact sciences, not even rocket science.

I have also mentioned that people try to fit scripture into a particular genre to better understand the events in the Bible, the problem is that scripture is testimony, or a witness to an event which may be acceptable in a court of law as evidence, but cannot be attributed to a genre. And as with all testimony, it is addressed to a specific audience for their need to understand a situation, and it varies according to each witness and to each audience. The only scripture we have in which prophets addressed a future audience is the Book of Mormon, all other prophets have addressed the people of their time, and we have modern day prophets who address us in our time. We will always need ancient scriptures to help us understand the Kingdom of God, we must always gain the prior knowledge before we can advance in our understanding, as knowledge is gained line upon line and precept upon precept.

Historians are finding lots of historical facts that are consistent in the Book of Mormon. Ancient Native Americans, before Columbus, were not just nomadic tribes living in tepees but lived in great cities with established trading routes. DNA mapping has shown Native American ancestry coming from the Mediterranean area possibly crossing the Atlantic Ocean by boat, rather than a natural land bridge crossing Siberia to Alaska. In 1960 a style of Hebrew poetry called *chiasmus* was discovered prominently through the Old Testament and later it was recognized in the Book of Mormon, as well. The Book of Mormon has also been attributed with proper Hebrew grammar similar to the Old Testament, instead of proper English grammar, and the Book of Ether contains a grammar style completely unique. These are all recent discoveries that Joseph Smith could not have been aware of while translating the gold plates.

Historical facts help us to understand events in history and confirm many of the things we already believe, but they do not make a religion true nor is true religion built on historical facts. True religion can only be built upon revelation. People always hope they can prove their religion correct through historical facts, but historical facts can be wrong just like any other science, and anyone can claim historical facts to support their beliefs.

When Moses wrote the book of Genesis, he did not write an historically or scientifically accurate account of the creation of the world, he was taken up in vision and shown all things from their beginnings laid out before him. He wrote those things down according to his own understanding and the understandings of his people. If Moses was an astronomer he may have written an entirely different account, or if he was a geologist, or a geneticist. But Moses spent 40 years of his life in Egypt learning to govern people and 40 years roaming the wilderness as a sheep herder, and he had to write what he saw in a way his people could understand. This is how all revelation is given. Some people say revelation is word for word dictation from God to a prophet, but they don't know how revelation is received because they don't receive it.

Chapter 27: Holiness to The Lord

Today I drove up to Castle Rock and sat for a while. It's just a great big chunk of basalt sticking up out the ground, doesn't even really look like a castle, but it does look like a mighty fortress standing tall to weather the test of time and the elements. There are quite a few mountains around here and most of them are pretty baron of trees, so you can see the formations of the land, it's kind of like a geologist's wonderland. They can get up in helicopters and planes and see for hundreds of miles around how the earth took its shape. This is one of my favorite places to be. I went into town the other night and walked along the main street where all the cars were cruising town with their loud mufflers and music, and people at the bars and restaurants, and all the flashing lights. It drove me half nuts in about fifteen minutes. But up here in the mountains and the trees I find peace and solitude. It's probably where God likes to sit and think, too.

I mentioned that common knowledge didn't have to be proven and that it was acceptable to believe what everyone else believes. This is contrary to any kind of holiness. The word "holy" means to be separate. The Holy Bible is a book separate from others, the holy temple is an edifice separate from the world, and a holy people are separate from worldliness. All things of true righteousness are different, peculiar, or set apart from the ways of the world. We can see how men have changed the Bible in ways to be more acceptable by the common people, and we can see how worldly religions change to conform to worldliness, but in order to grow closer to God we have to put distance between ourselves and Satan.

I'd like to mention one particular version of the Bible that's been in print since 2003. I could have brought it up in a previous chapter, but this is a special case, it goes beyond changing a few words to alter their meanings. It is titled *The Books of the Bible* and can be found at Biblica.com. You have to be specific about this because the internet has thousands of references to the various books in the Bible. This version of the Bible was completely redesigned and formatted without chapter heads or verses, and the columns were replaced with full page paragraphs without numbers. All of the like books were combined (1 & 2 Samuel, 1 & 2 Kings, 1 & 2 Chronicles, the four Gospels,) and rearranged in chronological order for a linear time line. It was designed to have more appearance to a novel than to scripture, to have more natural flow and ease of reading, so those who did not like reading the Bible would find this more enjoyable. It was designed to have a less harsh impact on those not living gospel standards. I imagine their intentions were good, but this is further altering sacred text according to the judgments of man, to make it less holy, or separated, from other books fabricated from the minds of mere mortal men. There is another version of the Bible simply titled *The Book,* published in 1999, as a New Living Translation Bible by Tyndale House Publishers, this is an easy to understand Bible designed for people who are new to the Bible or are unbelievers. The title of the book certainly doesn't undermine its purpose; the word "bible" comes from the Greek *ta biblia,* or the books. But taking its distinctive name away also takes away one of the traits that separate it from other books. Holiness is to be separate from worldliness, not become more common with it.

The free-for-all gospels and world religions will offer a certain degree of salvation for their faithful followers, but only the true gospel of Jesus Christ allows people the highest degree of Glory offered by our Heavenly Father, and following the commandments of Jesus Christ requires knowledge and understanding, commitment and diligence, and every possible effort to live in righteousness. We make ourselves holy and worthy to be in the presence of our Heavenly Father, exaltation is not freely given to us, we are to seek and strive after it. Where the effort is great the rewards should be great, the Celestial Kingdom is the reward for working harder than the others, it is the prize for coming in first place. All holiness is to put distance between the self and the adversary and draw closer to Christ. Repentance is to turn away from sin, baptism is to be washed clean of sin, and Sanctification allows continuous growth in spirituality until we are worthy to be with our Heavenly Father. The covenants we make in the temple allow us Celestial glory and put the greatest distance between us and Satan. Spreading the Gospel, perfecting the Saints and redeeming the dead are all acts of holiness.

In the Kingdom of Heaven people will be divided into degrees of glory according to their righteousness. This is a separation of the holy from the unholy. I can imagine the degrees of Glory being similar to the spheres of righteousness here on earth. The Celestial Kingdom would be like the holy temples, only those who follow the highest standards of the Gospel may be there, but they can access all other spheres around them. The Terrestrial Kingdom is like a worship house, like ours or any Christian worship house, or synagogue, or mosque, in which others who obey righteously according to the laws they've been given, and can also access other spheres except for the holy temples. The Telestial Kingdom is like the people of the world around us, obeying the laws of the land but not abiding any particular higher laws. And the outer darkness is like a state or federal prison, the inmates are confined because they have chosen not to follow laws and are agents unto themselves, they cannot access any spheres outside their own.

The ways of God are different than the ways of man and those who follow God will be different from other men. Written on the outside of every LDS temple is written the words *House of the Lord, Holiness to the Lord.* They are special places people can go to and separate themselves from the world and become closer to the Lord. A righteous people will be different, peculiar, and set apart from the rest of the world. People of the world try to make the Bible worldlier, and make their religions worldlier to accommodate worldly people, but their eternal rewards will not be that of a God who is separate from them.

Jesus Christ did not suffer the pains of hell, endure every temptation and attempt on his life, and rise above all things just to have a bunch of slackers take the thrones next to him. Those who hear His voice will come to Him, so we separate ourselves from the herd and come to him in righteousness, and leave the others to muddle as they see fit. He showed how much He cared, now we show how much we care, and we do everything we can to make His sacrifice worthwhile.

Chapter 28: Jesus, Save Us from Your Followers

There are times like today when I'm driving the water tanker around in frozen fog and ice covered roads, I struggle with all my might to chain up just to back up to the evaporation pit to unload, and I catch myself cussing like a sailor. If my mother was listening she'd wonder where she went wrong. I think of what a royal pain winter driving is and I wish to the high heavens the oil companies would go find something else to do over the holidays. Turns out, they did. They left all the flow back water for us to haul away. But then I sit in the cab and look over the snow blanketed hills, with little flecks of crystals glimmering in the sun, and watch a coyote high-tailing it over the ridge. I blasted my air horn but he was already on the move and I spooked a herd of deer out of the draw and watched them scamper across the meadow. I think it's a beautiful world and God made it just for me.

Today we redefine reality; 40 is the new 30, sensitivity is the new macho, feminism is the new feminine, politics is the new prejudice, and obnoxiousness is the new outspoken. It seems we can't view anything in the media where people are not making complete asses of themselves in defense of their beliefs. It's called free speech. Freedom from restraint is the new freedom from responsibility. As time draws closer to the Second Coming, worldly ways draw farther from Godly ways. Many Christians are following suit with the worldly trends to become more aggressive, while Mormons continue following the Lord's commission to be good examples, and to send missionaries throughout the world.

Presently, there are people who take to the streets interviewing passers-by on Gospel centered issues. But these interviews are more like interrogations. First, they set up filming equipment; cameras, lights, sound, and crew. Then they ask incriminating questions. Are you a good person? Have you ever lied, looked upon a person with lust, stolen, gotten angry, or taken the Lord's name in vain? Once the person has answered yes to each question the interviewer unabashedly accuses them of being a liar, whoremonger, thief, murderer and blasphemer. Then they ask if that person believes they will be received into heaven. Finally they start cramming their version of the Gospel down their victim who is desperately struggling to maintain a shred of dignity in front of the camera. The system is quite simple. First, use the video camera, crew members, and an interviewer to put a person on the spot; so they automatically feel self-conscious. Then play head games; attack their hope of salvation or their sense of understanding. Make them question their own certainty so they don't question the interviewer. Put the person on the defense so he can take control of the conversation, frustrate them so they can't think straight, and compromise their emotional stability so their fight or flight instincts kick in. These people attack in a mental and emotional way yet claim to be ministers of God witnessing to non-believers. Similarly, some sinister ministers have their own TV shows and radio programs where they scarcely do anything but badger people's beliefs. If anyone gets mad at their obnoxiousness then they accuse people of hating God and being blind to the enlightenment of the Gospel. They are the wolves in sheep's clothing we are warned about.

We have a completely different approach. We are encouraged to befriend non-members and be living examples of the principles of the Gospel. We try to be the living proof that our Church is not a bunch of wild-eyed cultists we're accused of. We try to be the friends we'd like to have, we try to be the ministers and teachers we'd like to meet, and we try to be the changes we'd like to see in others. When people feel safe and secure around us they will inquire about us and we can be the missionaries President David

O. McKay commanded us to be. After several Latter-day Saints pass through these people's lives and kindly take part in preparing the soil, the seeds can be planted. Call in the missionaries.

Our missionaries are the most visible representatives of our Church. They are well-dressed young men and women walking the streets of almost any city, town or community in pairs and talking to people on the streets or knocking on doors. Nearly all other members of the Church blend perfectly with their environment taking on jobs and professions right along with the people who surround them. Missionaries usually meet with people in the privacy of their own homes where they feel safe and secure and can define the terms and conditions of the meeting. If at any time, as it's been done many times, people do not want the missionaries in their homes they can oust them as they see fit. They can make threats with fire arms or sick dogs (or their local pastors) on them, but whatever the case, we meet with people on their own terms. We offer people the opportunity to learn more and draw closer to our Heavenly Father through Jesus Christ. We offer the Book of Mormon as another testament of Jesus Christ so that they can read, ponder and pray about. We invite them to our worship houses so they can see for themselves who Mormons are and what we are about. We invite them to social parties so they can meet new people and make friends. Most people have an enjoyable experience, some actually stay with us, others it takes longer and some never do. But no matter what, we keep working with them, because it is our obligation to help our fellow man return to our Heavenly Father.

In contrast to other methods that have been shown to be damaging and destructive, our methods still work the best. When we live by the principles of the Gospel we know to be true, others will follow suit as they are drawn to those truths, and can start to see the deception around them. Those of the world will follow worldly ways, and so will Christian ministers not of God, because they see what is effective in the world and do the same things.

Many Christians today have followed the same aggressive and obnoxious trends as mass media, but Latter-day Saints hold to the principles taught by the Savior, and send out missionaries to meet with people face to face in the meek and gentle manners they've always been taught.

These aggressive and forceful methods are not the ways all Christian pastors and teachers conduct themselves, most are model Christians who are everything we could expect a Christian to be; sweet natured, kind and courteous, and holding a genuine concern for the well-being of their fellow man. Of all the good ecclesiastical leaders, men and women, throughout the world teaching righteousness and goodness to their neighbors, there are a few wing-nuts who give everyone a bad name. There is a special place in the eternities reserved for them.

Chapter 29: Reformation and Revelation

I recently started work in Williston, North Dakota, which is sort of a boom town because of the oil drilling the last few years. People have come from all over the country to find work here. There are semi-trucks and pick-ups all over the place in a mad dash to get somewhere. I haven't heard anyone say *You're darned tootin',* probably because nobody around here is from around here. Then I see a man in ragged clothes holding a cardboard sign that says, *Just need work.* Now, that is something that doesn't make sense to me. Being in a town like this and not finding work is like being at a spice mill and not finding a pepper grinder.

We tend to think of reformation as the Protestant separation from the Catholic Church in the 1500's. Religious reformation is taking the belief structure of an already existing system and changing it to suit the needs of the people...or the governing body. We know that true religion does not come from reformation but from revelation. Reformation has been in effect since the days of Adam and has evolved into some of the major world religions, Christian reformation began during the ministry of the early Apostles, and the Restoration of the Gospel through Joseph Smith has demonstrated how true religion is established.

We know that Adam had a perfect knowledge of the Father and the Son and through time he was given the principles of the Gospel and also taught them to his children, thus the earliest known reformation from true doctrine was Cain's effort to offer an unsatisfactory sacrifice *(Gen. 4:2-4.)* The oldest religion still in existence and being practiced today is Hinduism, supposedly dating back a million years, but may go back to the Tower of Babel when the nations and tongues were divided. Buddhism is a fairly recent spin-off of Hinduism from about 500 BC. Each of the eastern religions has been a modification of an existing religion separated by geology, time and developing cultures. The western religions have been similar. Judaism has kept most of its reformation within its own bounds and it has only been in recent years that other branches have developed. Christianity branched off from Judaism and Islam from Christianity about 500 AD.

Christian reformation began during the mission of the Apostles; in fact, the epistles of Peter, James, John, and Paul were efforts to correct the teachings and practices of various churches in the regions that were already going astray. As early as the 100's, after the deaths of the Apostles, we see the strong influence of Greek mythology and the dissolving priesthood structure. Some of the concepts being introduced and argued were Docetism, Aryanism, Trinitarianism, and dualistic beliefs. By the 300's there was so much controversy and conflict over the variations of the gospel that efforts to quell the disputes resulted in Christianity being adopted as a national religion in Armenia in 301, Ethiopia in 325, Georgia in 337, and Rome in 380 AD. In 325 AD the Emperor Constantine gathered his council in Nicaea and determined that Trinitarian Christianity would be the gospel concerning the Godhead and established the Catholic Church, their official proclamation became known as the Nicene Creed and is still adhered to by nearly all Christians; Orthodox and Protestant. Through time bishops of the Church wrote doctrines meant to explain issues concerning the Gospel and their standardized doctrines became known as orthodoxy, or *true belief*. Constantine played an active role in the development of Christianity as he supported the Church financially, built various basilicas, granted privileges to clergy, promoted Christians to high ranking offices, and returned confiscated property. In the mid-5th century the Eastern Orthodox and the Oriental Orthodox Churches branched off. Monastic Churches evolved and were headed by hermit monks; nunneries were particularly popular with the ladies. Westward expansion and rule of the Ottoman Empire in the east caused many changes in the Church and by the 1500's Protestant reformation was on.

In the spring of 1820, Joseph Smith, Jr. knelt in a small wooded grove near Palmyra, New York to pray for guidance in his pursuit for true religion, to his astonishment one of the most remarkable events in recorded history happened. God the Father and His son Jesus Christ appeared to him and told him not to join any of the existing churches of the day as their traditions and creeds were completely wrong. Joseph never went to the woods expecting an open vision, nor did he expect what he was told, but his eye witness account changed over a thousand years of theology and tradition in a way that no mortal mind could imagine. Joseph had other open visions of ministering angels, past prophets, degrees of glory, and future events. He was the first since New Testament times to demonstrate the spiritual gifts of visions, prophecy, healing, tongues, and seership, thus showing that these were not just mythical powers given to ancient prophets but gifts given to God's righteous people to do His work. He was given Priesthood authority and Keys directly from those prominent men who held them last, resurrected and translated men who took those things with them when they left this world, those things necessary to operate God's true Church. He was given new doctrine on how to establish the true Church and how to prepare the people of this day for the Second Coming. At no time has the Lord ever revealed that He would no longer work in these ways.

The point of this chapter is to demonstrate that reformation has always been in effect and has been the most used method in establishing religion. Reformation is not a principle of the Gospel; it is not taught in the Bible or demonstrated in righteousness, it's not even mentioned, whereas *revelation* and *restoration* are. Cain was the first person to make radical changes in religion and enforce them with violence, Protestant reformation was an effort to change the Catholic Church but resulted in completely new branches of Christianity, but the restoration of the Gospel through revelation has brought back the ways of God to mankind.

The Christian reformers; Johannes (Jan or John) Hus, John Calvin, Martin Luther, John Wycliffe, William Tyndale, John Knox, Huldrych Zwingli and many others felt the need to resist the oppression of the day and strive to make the Bible and other truths available to all people, break the bands of State governed church, and cause people to strive for religious freedom. They paved the way for the Restored Gospel to come to fruition. Because of their works, dedication, and sacrifices we know the early Christian reformers have earned their places in the highest heavens...plus we did their temple work.

Chapter 30: Correct Theology

About half way up Heart Mountain, on a hike an old man like me shouldn't have gone on without the aid of my old Jeep, I found some sea shells. I'm not very keen on identifying what kind of shells they are but I'm sure there's an "app" on somebody's smart phone that can identify it. Signs of marine life on a desert mountain are not so unusual, we find this all over the western U.S., and it's been determined that all of the central North America was under sea at one time. What gets me is these shells are not fossilized. They're just dried up old shells and the dirt pours right out of them. I'm just not so sure this area was covered by a shallow sea 2.5 million years ago; it's a big number for such little dried up shell. It's okay, geologists still haven't figured out how Heart Mountain got there in the first place.

People say that in order to have true Christianity you must have correct theology. Naturally, theology is extracted from the Bible, which currently is printed in 30 variations in the English language translated from 56,000 variations of Greek texts, and the World Christian Encyclopedia has identified about 33,000 different Christian denominations worldwide and 2.5 billion Christians. So somebody's gotta have it right, right? Fact is, there can be millions of false churches in the world but there can only be one that is true. Theology has been expanded to be the widest used method of learning religion, and many theologians would like to believe that higher knowledge comes from higher education, but it isn't theology that makes a religion true.

Theology is a systematic and rational study of religion. In a sense it is a scientific approach to the nature of religious truths, but since the sciences usually involve systematic testing to get quantifiable results, theology is more of a philosophy. Theologians usually receive special training in religious studies from universities, schools of divinity or seminary. Theology and religious studies are not the same creatures; religious scholars draw upon multiple disciplines including anthropology, sociology, psychology, philosophy, and history to understand the significance of religion in society. Most men, and some women now, in the ministries of Catholic and Protestant churches have received formal educations in the field of religion to aid their ministries, and their degrees add credibility to their status as ministers. Pastors use various forms of analysis and argument to help understand, explain, critique and defend religious topics. Some of these arguments are based on philosophical, ethnographic, historical and spiritual forms of analysis. Universities have been set up for the teaching of religion since the early days of the Catholic Church and have been central in developing theology through the middle ages. That tradition has been passed down through the Protestant churches as well. Ministers learn the fine art of preaching, prayer and assembling the congregations for worship and social activities. But I have found something absolutely crucial to understand; while many religions base their knowledge and practices on theology, theology is not religion *(1 Cor. 2:9-14.)*

As Latter-day Saints we tend to thumb our noses at those who feel you need a college degree to understand the Kingdom of Heaven. Granted we have our Church owned universities of higher learning; Brigham Young University in Provo, Utah, BYU of Idaho (the Y of I,) and BYU of Hawaii, among other community and business colleges, and we have institute schools set up near just about every college in the country so our youths can receive credit in their study fields. We have many people schooled in religion to direct and teach in these institutes. But higher learning is not required to understand the mysteries of God, Priesthood authority delivers that, and every worthy male member of the Church is given Priesthood authority. We know that the knowledge of the Kingdom of Heaven is tied directly to the Melchizedek Priesthood. Very few of our General Authorities have higher education in the theological fields, seldom do our Bishops or Stake leaders, and neither do I. It's rumored that Joseph Smith had the education equivalent to an 8th grader; essentially he could read, write and do basic math, and all home schooled.

Theology seems to be a requirement in most Christianity, but it is not a principle of the Gospel, not any more than "authority of the scriptures." Reasoning out principles of the Gospel is a commandment,*Come now, and let us reason together, saith the LORD: though your sins be as scarlet, they shall be as white as snow; though they be red like crimson, they shall be as wool (Isaiah 1:18.)* Again Jesus himself said; *For where two or three are gathered together in my name, there am I in the midst of them (Matt. 18:20.)* This is the reason we have meeting houses where we can worship and study together. The principles of the Gospel are extremely broad to apply to all people, but we meet to discuss these principles and share stories and testimonies of how they can be applied to the individual. We are advised by our general authorities to avoid *intellectualizing* the Gospel, or more specifically, to ignore the spiritual significance of doctrine through excessive intellectual or abstract explanation. We don't want to philosophize its practical applications. We don't want to take the term *question everything* from curiosity, understanding, and enlightenment to become bold and outright defiance. No successful religion is without meaning, or the group of values (principles put to action) which people find essential for a sense of wholeness or completion, and it is the Gospel of Jesus Christ which gives us that meaning.

The notion of having correct theology to be a true Christian is a whole lot of hooey. Theology cannot produce a true religion, only revelation can do that. The study of God through a system of reason and logic is a major part of almost every Christian church around, but higher learning is not the key to understanding the gospel, and we don't use theology as a replacement for the true means of establishing a true religion; revelation.

Nothing is more important than the Gospel of Jesus Christ or the revelations we get from it. Where there is no revelation there is no Gospel. *Beware lest any man spoil you through philosophy and vain deceit, after the tradition of men, after the rudiments of the world, and not after Christ. (Col. 2:8) For I neither received it of man, neither was I taught it, but by the revelation of Jesus Christ. (Gal. 1:12)*

Chapter 31: Hindsight Bias

The more sand has escaped from the hourglass of our life, the clearer we should see through it. *Jean Paul Satre.* Last winter I spent a day filling frac tanks and when I finished I had the mind to drain my trailer so the valves wouldn't freeze over-night. I promptly grabbed the valve handle, stepped slightly to the side to avoid getting water all over me, and opened it up. A burst of water shot passed me for fifty yards. That trailer had a jet stream like a booster rocket and I realized I forgot to shut off the pump and depressurize the tank. Somehow, after doing a repetitious job for several months the brain decided to just skip a few steps. Looking back I can clearly see it wasn't a good idea and fortunately nobody was hurt, in fact, nobody was even around to see it so my silly pride wasn't at risk. If I hadn't stepped to the side of the valve opening I would have been blasted into the next county trying to thumb a ride back, people would ask what happened and why I was all wet, and I'd say I don't want to talk about it.

Hindsight bias is the culprit for much false doctrine. This is the inclination to view events that have already happened with the notion the results could have been predicted before they took place. It is the erroneous assumption to recognize the problems of a situation when those present could not foresee the event. We think we're smart because we knew it all along. All biasness is based on hindsight. Hindsight bias is a condition common in the human race, and many religious leaders through time have adopted hindsight bias as a primary mode of establishing doctrine, but we can see that the principles of the Gospel are designed to help people overcome this root of all prejudice.

Hindsight bias is a real psychological issue common among ordinary people, we all look back and realize how stupid we were, but in some cases it can cause memory distortion in recollecting and reconstructing content that can lead to false conclusions. In the early '70's, psychologists noticed that many clinical doctors were making comments overestimating their abilities to foresee the outcomes of particular cases as if they had known the problems all along. So they began to study and found this to be the case everywhere they went. This concept also applies to people changing their opinions after new information is provided and claiming it to be their original views. Hindsight can affect judgment when making decisions as people will often side with a scenario that has some kind of past connection or familiarity, and that decision is supported by the person's own interpretation. The understanding of causes in events is also greatly affected by hindsight. When an event goes unexpected people will often draw upon their own experiences to make sense of why things happened unexpectedly, possibly to feel more positive about the outcome or themselves for not knowing in the first place.

Hindsight bias in religion has led to the greatest deceptions in history. It is so interwoven with the sermons of ministers that people believe this is how sermons should be presented. Nearly every reference to the Bible is an effort to analyze the situation from thousands of years ago and use modern understanding to critique it. Theology can only be developed through hindsight bias. Orthodoxy can only be established through hindsight bias. Evaluating the present human condition based solely on ancient scripture can only be done through hindsight bias. It is no wonder theologians come up with so many goofy concepts in religion, and it's no wonder how they can be so far off. It is the pride of hindsight that ministers began telling people that prophets were no longer needed to guide people, that they were far more righteous and obedient than people of old, and that everything God wants us to know is already in the Bible. It was the pride of hindsight that caused many ancient Jews to reject Jesus Christ and the new covenant claiming to be the children of Abraham and having the

Law of Moses, and it is that same hindsight that causes people today to reject modern day prophets and new scripture claiming to be Christians and having the Bible. Even historians distort truth when they assume ancient people were less intelligent than people of today, and they underestimate their capabilities from back then, and misjudge our present conditions.

Hindsight has its practical side as a learning tool as we gain experience in life and learn to make better choices. But revelation has given us an eternal perspective on life. We are given truth concerning all things spiritual to understand the past, present and future. With revelation, hindsight becomes interpolation, as inspiration combines with experience to create a fuller understanding. It has been proven in psychological testing that the only way to eliminate hindsight bias is to increase accountability in people's actions. Repentance and charity are by far the best ways for people to quit blaming themselves or others for circumstances beyond their control. People are less subject to hindsight bias when they focus on positive outcomes, become less attached to the actual outcomes, and consider alternative lines of reasoning for resolving problems. Forgiveness is an all-important remedy for hindsight bias. All of the principles of the Gospel are designed to help people overcome their natural tendencies to dwell on the past. Faith, hope and charity are all tools to thrust people forward to a brighter future, our Savior told us these things because He knew people would get bogged down with the past, and He wanted us to learn how to move on to a happier life.

I rode in a truck with a man who had issues with Mormons and knew several that he didn't like, naturally he told me all about them, and I told him that a few bad experiences could make a person sour. In time we developed a good friendship, but I didn't let his biasness affect me, and soon his attitude changed. All our past experiences have an effect on how we view people and we seem to dwell the most on the bad ones. It's a common problem with the human condition, and religious leaders have let hindsight bias govern much of their teachings, but with a true understanding of the Gospel we see that an eye equal to God's will overcome all biasness.

Knowing and understanding hindsight bias is as crucial to spiritual growth as knowing the existence of God. Just like money is the root of all evil, we can say hindsight bias is the root of all prejudice. Probably the worst thing about hindsight bias is that so much theology is based on it, the second worst is that people can hardly make rational decisions without it.

Chapter 32: Prove All Things

In the first chapter I talked about the anthropomorphic God and how His human qualities give Him a unique perspective on the human condition and helps us to recognize our potential to be like Him. Today was Father's Day, and while I thought some of my Dad who passed away a few years ago, I thought more about my Heavenly Father and how I long at times to be in His presence again. I think that as human beings we are inherently lonely, in spite of the friends we might make or the loves which we share, I think that most of us feel we are strangers in this world and so out of place in. Somehow, we can't get it out of our heads that there is something greater out there, beyond this world that if we just hold on to our sanity long enough, we might have richer rewards. It's called hope.

The power of suggestion is an amazing thing. For instance, we are boldly and blatantly told we cannot prove the existence of God, and we graciously concede. Even the very definition of *faith* has included the term: *to believe without proof.* Yet, it is a commandment right along with praying and giving thanks, we are to *Prove all things (1 Thes. 5:21.)* We must understand what proof is, what can be accepted as proof, and then we can show how all things can be proven.

People tend to go with the old "scientific proof" as the basis of their arguments, but I can assure you they have not looked into the matter with any degree of intent, and they simply use it as an excuse or defense, probably because they haven't yet look into the matter. The purpose of science is very simple; to explain phenomena. A phenomenon is anything that excites people's interests and can be considered extraordinary and marvelous. Undoubtedly, God would be phenomenal. But then philosophy—to establish truth through logic and reasoning, and theology—to understand God through logic and reasoning, would be shooting for the same goal. But science is different; it establishes real and solid evidence, right? *General Theory* is a broad view of events used to predict patterns in phenomena, such as celestial events, geologic processes, weather forecasts, economic or political shifts, etc. Theories use mathematical models to quantify events and predict outcomes but follow very few scientific laws, because astronomy and geology often have events that happen too slowly to be observed, and the weather and people have too many variables to be consistent. Furthermore, astronomy and geology are often based on *uniformitarianism,* or the notion that what we see happening now has always been happening the same way, it does not consider catastrophism. Heart Mountain in Wyoming is the perfect exception to uniformitarianism. Scientific theories are often called working theories because they are subject to change as new evidence is found, sort of "work in progress" theories. *Specific Theory* is a more localized and personal effort in which specialists can work, using established knowledge to perform a function. Doctors use specific theories to diagnose illnesses and recommend treatment, chemists use specific theories to connect the science of atoms with other natural sciences such as geology and biology, engineers figure out how to build things, cooks use recipes, mechanics troubleshoot, etc., we all use specific theories in everyday life without even thinking about it, even when I break out a map to plan a road trip I'm using specific theory. *Scientific Law* does not explain phenomena; it is simply reduction and repeated observation. Scientific law is the basis of all science but it is extremely limited and rigid, and can only be applied and demonstrated in controlled and exacting conditions, and without those controlled and exacting conditions the law is refuted by innumerable variables, like herding cats. For every way to prove something right there are thousands of ways to prove it wrong. Observation always trumps theory. Even the defining characteristic of a scientific theory is whether it can be falsified. None of the sciences are exact sciences. This is the unconditional term of reality; if it cannot be proven wrong it cannot be real. So, where are we expected to find God in all of this? Can we use any of this to fulfill the commandment to prove all things?

My friends, there is another form of proof, one that works within us. A form that takes place beyond the confines of scientific law and not limited to the imaginations of men, that every reasonable person can recognize regardless of their education or social status, and one that even the smallest of children can understand. It is the personal witness or experience, *the testimony,* which is admissible in any court of law as evidence. More people are convicted or exonerated based on eye witness accounts than any forensic evidence. People make thousands of decisions each day using their own experiences rather than scientific data. It is the personal experience that defines reality for each individual and it is the shared experience that offers testimony. A shared experience is proof of a truth. If I burn my hand and whack my elbow while working on the Jeep, do I need to postulate a scientific theory or refer to a scientific law to convince somebody that it flippin' hurts? Anyone who has burnt themselves knows exactly what I feel. We're all here for the experience of mortality, and because of the experiences we gain we can relate to those having similar experiences, so we have proof of reality within us.

This is precisely the way God works. It is our life's experiences that testify of God's existence. The beautiful thing is; it's all personal and individual, what may be compelling evidence for me may not be evidence for someone else. Our Heavenly Father knows exactly what works for each of us and He can supply that knowledge, that is why the Bible is not evidence of God's existence, but a manifestation of the Holy Ghost is *(John 15:26.)* That is why person-to-person discussions are more effective than controlled experiments. This is why we invite friends to go to Church and other related activities with us. This is why we ask people to read the Book of Mormon, to ponder and pray about it, so they can learn for themselves of its truths. There isn't anyone in the Church who insists people take our words to be matter of facts. Follow the commandments of God and see for yourself how they work, obey the teachings of Jesus Christ to see how they become the fabric of morality and the values to live by, and go to the temple to feel the love of God that no words can describe. The knowledge of God is a shared experience which proves His existence. Anyone who wants to know can know. And this is how we can know the truth of all things.

I mentioned that observation always trumps theory, so we can confidently say that all scientific proof is established through personal witness. To believe in God is a matter of choice, not proof. The scientific fields have their purposes but at no point have they been declared tools for engaging the divine, the proof of God's existence lies within each of us and we all can gain a knowledge and testimony that He really is there.

It is the most unreasonable demand that has ever rolled off the tongues of mockers. When we want to look at the stars we build telescopes, we have satellites looking deep into space, and we now have one specially made to look for planets orbiting other stars. When we want to see something really tiny we build microscopes. When we want to smash atoms together we build a particle accelerator. So, what technology has been developed to find God? Does anyone have a clue where to start? By far the best efforts of anyone with the best of intentions have produced resounding questionable results. Nobody has been able to figure out how to use the scientific fields to find God any more than figuring out how to use a jack-hammer to cut diamonds. God can only be known through revelation and He gives His mind and will to any *receptive* mortals as He sees fit.

Chapter 33: What the Prophet Said

It doesn't seem that long ago somebody asked what made my Church so different from others; I said we had a true and living prophet and that he had just spoke in General Conference. In the most enthusiastic way they asked what he said, and I just stood there with a stupid look on my face. Ironically, General Conference came up again right about the time I'm bringing this masterful manuscript to a close, but this time I took notes.

Having no other record at present of the Prophet's words other than those notes, I will attempt to reconstruct some of those things from the past two days. 31 March 2012, Saturday morning session: President Thomas S. Monson welcomed all those watching or listening and mentioned that we were all here to learn and gain incentive to change, oppose evil, and that the great cause of the Gospel continues forward through the world. He quoted the Thirteenth Article of Faith *If there is anything virtuous, lovely, or of good report or praiseworthy, we seek after these things.* He invited all to come to be instructed and inspired and wanted all to know that God is mindful to us.

31 March 2012, Priesthood session: President Monson addressed the body of Priesthood holders, over 20,000 present in the Conference Center, and shared some of the teachings of past Presidents of the Church. He affirmed that the Priesthood was eternal and was the power of God given to man, that it is the Government of God, and the agency by which all things in heaven and on earth are done. He also mentioned that opportunity was coupled with responsibility and duty. The war on the souls of men continues unabated and Priesthood holders have a call to duty to

fight that war. We must always be on the Lord's errand, we must discern what the Lord wants from us, then use the Priesthood to magnify our efforts and callings. He closed in saying that if we do not magnify our callings the Lord will hold us responsible for the souls not saved.

1 April 2012, Sunday morning session: President Monson closed the session: He talked of eternal truths and placing Gospel Principles as a priority in life. He lamented the idea that people these days are always in such a hurry, in an endless stream of cars and airplanes taking people where they have to be, and that everyday issues lose their significance in times of crisis. He told of a woman who was obsessive about her possessions and her time but when diagnosed with a terminal illness vowed to dedicate her time and efforts to the Gospel. Limited time often draws people to re-evaluate priorities toward the spiritual rather than the worldly. He mentioned the important questions in life, as *Where did we come from? Why are we here? Where do we go after this life?* Then he recalled the testament of Paul on Mars Hill in the Book of Hebrews; that we are literally begotten of God and that heaven lies about us in our infancy. Mortality is a time of testing and opportunity, that we are under the hard task master called *experience,* and that this is the time for us to qualify for the Highest mansion. God did not send us here to fail, but to succeed greatly. He told the story of a toy boat race down the Provo River as each of the little boats was subject to the currents with no rudders or power to control them. We have divine guidance in the scriptures, living prophets, and the Holy Ghost to help guide us back to our Heavenly Father. He talked of a man whose wife had died, and the man concluded that death was not what anyone would expect, that it was more like stepping into another room. The presence of God is where we desire to dwell and our Heavenly Father rejoices for those who keep His commandments.

1 April 1012, Sunday afternoon session: President Monson's final words in Conference. He expressed gratitude for the touching

testimonies of all those who spoke at the conference, the beautiful music, the talents behind the scenes, to those released from their callings, and support for those newly called. Acknowledged the unprecedented coverage broadcast worldwide. Expressed God's love for us, admonished us to pray always and great shall be our blessings. He advised families to settle disputes and avoid contention, and our homes would be filled with love. He mentioned that all prophets are subject to mortal infirmities, always desire to do God's will, and invoke blessings for the betterment of the people. End.

By no means are these statements word-for-word as they rolled of the tongue of our prophet, I don't have the ability to dictate fast enough, but these are the essences of what the prophet taught. Soon the exact sermons will be published in print, audio CD, and on digital video disks, and people can know exactly what the prophet said. But whether we have the exact words or just some jotted notes, it is far more important that we understand what is said and that we apply them in our lives and this is the way all testimonies from prophets ancient and modern should be taken. It makes me wonder if this isn't how many original Bible texts were written, just notes quickly jotted down in Hebrew or Aramic shorthand, and then reconstructed later for publication.

I leave this testimony, that we have a true and living Prophet on the earth today presiding over the only true Church of Jesus Christ, that as the glorious work of the Gospel presses forward Satan loses his grip on the world, and that as we follow the counsels of the Prophet, Satan loses his grip on us. As a Priesthood holder I know that the heavens are unlocked and inspiration pours out upon the righteous throughout the world. The Second Coming is soon at hand, but not right now, there are still some things that need to be done. I can think of no greater time to be alive in the world, and I am thankful for that. In the name of Jesus Christ, amen.